THE RATIONALE FOR NATO

AEI-Hoover
policy studies

The studies in this series are issued jointly
by the American Enterprise Institute
for Public Policy Research and the Hoover
Institution on War, Revolution and Peace.
They are designed to focus on
policy problems of current and future interest,
to set forth the factors underlying
these problems and to evaluate
courses of action available to policymakers.
The views expressed in these studies
are those of the authors and do not necessarily
reflect the views of the staff, officers
or members of the governing boards of
AEI or the Hoover Institution.

THE RATIONALE
FOR NATO

European collective security— past and future

Morton A. Kaplan

American Enterprise Institute for Public Policy Research
Washington, D. C.

Hoover Institution on War, Revolution and Peace
Stanford University, Stanford California

AEI-Hoover Policy Study 8, August 1973
(Hoover Institution Studies 43)

ISBN 0-8447-3107-2
Library of Congress Catalog Card No. L.C. 73-85711

Printed in United States of America

Contents

Preface

This short book presents a proposal for a dissuasion strategy for NATO. Some readers may ask, "Why will not the old strategies do?" or "Why need we persist with a cold war invention?" As these points cannot be ignored, we have said something about them. But, as they are not the center of our concern, we have not made them the subject of highly detailed analyses or definitive historical inquiries.

Thus we will briefly recall the postwar situation, the onset of the cold war, the formation of NATO, its early history, and its present situation. Only in dealing with France and German rearmament do we resort to any detail. Even in this instance the detail is not designed to reveal the complexities of the issues or of national motivations. We are concerned only to impress upon the reader the sense of forced and resentful compliance with which the French responded to an American will that was imperial, even if also benevolent.

Recall of this aspect of the past is relevant to the present. Americans have a tendency to confuse support of U.S. policy with morality and intelligence. They tend to be deaf to the views of others and to ascribe any opposition to ill will or obstinacy. If we are to reinvigorate NATO in a world in which the United States is no longer the dominant power, we must become sensitive to the fact that other nations have views and interests that differ from ours. Our capacity to persuade is now more important than our capacity to compel acquiescence.

Phillip Karber and Charles Wassof of Braddock, Dunn, and McDonald were associated with me in developing the dissuasion strategy. It is presented here in the form in which I would advocate it.

Morton A. Kaplan

1

Collapse of the Wartime Alliance

NATO has been called one of the grandest inventions of modern political statesmanship. Many believe that the policies that produced the Truman Doctrine, the Marshall Plan, and NATO saved Europe from communism and preserved the prospects for democracy in the world.[1] Radical revisionists charge that NATO was cleverly designed by cold war imperialists to obscure an American drive for world domination.[2] More moderate critics characterize NATO as a blunder that deepened the cold war and that made more difficult the peaceful resolution of differences between the West and the Communist world. Reasoned inquiry into these claims and charges requires insight into the problems and perspectives of the leaders of the victorious coalition during the closing stages of the Second World War.

Leadership and War Diplomacy

At the end of the Second World War the United States was led by a President who had neither participated in nor been informed of the decisions in the major war conferences or the Manhattan Project. Harry S. Truman assumed office upon the sudden death of Franklin D. Roosevelt without any preparation for his new role. In addition, the United States was just emerging from an isolationism that was based on simplistic views of international politics and very sanguine expectations concerning our Soviet ally. The American public and many of its leaders

---

[1] For selected references, see bibliography below, p. 91.

[2] Ibid., p. 92.

3

were of a mind that was too far divorced from the pragmatics of actual decisions to permit a coherent synthesis of intellectual understanding and action. Many, including important United States senators, expected that major postwar problems could and should be solved by the United Nations.[3]

The Soviet Union was led by a cantankerously suspicious dictator with little direct experience of foreign countries in general and of Western states in particular. The great experienced leader of the British nation, Winston Churchill, was repudiated by his own public upon the conclusion of the European phase of the Second World War. In any event, he led a nation whose dependency on the United States allowed little freedom of action.

In large part, the situation that confronted American leaders in the concluding phases of the war was the product of their apolitical conduct of the war. The New Deal had been displaced by "Dr. Win-the-War." America's wartime leaders had understood this term almost literally. They ignored the extensive relationships that would necessarily exist between decisions made during the war and the pattern of postwar politics. For instance, the United States had refused to bring leverage against the Soviet Union for a Polish settlement at a time when American aid was essential to Soviet survival and before the Soviet Union had occupied Poland.[4] Even at the close of the war, Truman, upon the advice of Generals Eisenhower and Marshall, had refused to permit American armies to plunge toward Berlin—a course of action strongly advocated by Churchill—although such a move would have permitted the United States to bargain for concessions with respect either to Poland or Berlin in return for Western allied withdrawal to the agreed-upon occupation lines.[5] Contrary voices were beginning to be heard in the American government and these began to affect U.S. objectives in the Pacific. How-

---

[3] This became fully manifest in Senator Arthur Vandenberg's modifications of the early postwar Truman programs and in popular revulsion against Churchill's Fulton, Missouri speech of March 1946. He was soundly denounced, largely on grounds related to the U.N., by virtually all shades of important opinion. Of the major political figures of the day, only Thomas E. Dewey came to his public defense. See Gabriel Almond, *The American People and Foreign Policy* (New York: Praeger Publishers, Inc., 1960), pp. 29-68, for a discussion of American character and foreign policy.

[4] John L. Snell, ed., *The Meaning of Yalta: Big Three Diplomacy and the New Balance of Power* (Baton Rouge: Louisiana State University Press, 1956), pp. 86-88.

[5] Harry S. Truman, *Memoirs: Year of Decisions,* vol. 1 (Garden City, N. Y.: Doubleday and Co., 1955), pp. 212-14.

ever, these changes were merely variations on a fairly consistent theme: an apolitical, ahistorical, moralistic, and legalistic approach to international politics.

The American View of World Politics

The Roosevelt administration did not think of itself as abstractly idealistic. Franklin Roosevelt believed he understood the errors of the past and that he was acting to avoid their repetition. He assessed the reasons for the failures of the League of Nations, the costs resulting from American isolationism in the interwar period, and the measures required to prevent another brutal outbreak of world war. The war, he believed, had resulted from the aggressive designs of fascist dictatorships. Therefore, the war must be total so that the fascist nations could be reconstructed as democratic and peace-loving. The war had occurred because the League of Nations had failed and because no alliance of peace-loving nations had existed to stand up to the aggressive fascist powers. Therefore, to avoid the failures of the league, Roosevelt wanted a United Nations derived from the wartime alliance, with its enforcement actions based on the concerted police activities of the major victorious nations. Roosevelt was convinced that if the unity of these powers dissolved, then the world would face again the specter of fascism and world war. For this reason, he considered cooperation with the Russians an essential goal.[6]

If Roosevelt and his closest advisers saw themselves as realists, they nonetheless failed to perceive that differences in social and political systems, or in history and the perception of problems, might legitimately cause major conflicts of interest between Russia and the Western powers. If each side was honest and sincere, they thought, the desired objectives, including national self-determination in Europe, could be achieved.

American leaders found activities inconsistent with their postwar objectives difficult to understand. Incapable of seeing the potential conflict between genuinely independent governments in eastern Europe and governments friendly to the Soviet Union, they deplored Soviet actions in eastern Europe. As a consequence of the American leaders'

---

[6] William Reitzel, Morton A. Kaplan, and Constance G. Coblenz, *United States Foreign Policy: 1945-1955* (Washington, D. C.: The Brookings Institution, 1956), pp. 24-27. Also, see Edward R. Stettinius, Jr., *Roosevelt and the Russians: The Yalta Conference,* ed. Walter Johnson (Garden City, N. Y.: Doubleday and Co., 1949), p. 188.

investment in their hopes for the postwar order, at first they refused to recognize the Russian objectives for what they were, although Stalin had made little secret of them.[7] When the evidence began to build up, they were forced to despair for their grand design. And, if it would not work, it was difficult for them to interpret Soviet behavior in terms of security calculations. Eventually, although reluctantly and slowly, Americans came around to the view that Russian behavior was malevolent.

However, until this change did occur, even such conservative Americans as Senator Arthur Vanderberg continued to think that Russians were merely rude Americans who, confronted by plain talk and forceful opposition, would listen to reason. For instance, Representative Karl Mundt argued that negotiations between Americans and Russians would proceed much better if the United States did not act in concert with the British:

> We should . . . arrange soon a conference between the Big Two. Why? . . . Because . . . we have three of them sitting around the conference table—Churchill, Roosevelt, Stalin— now Stalin, Attlee, and Truman perhaps. On the way over Roosevelt and Churchill conferred together, and on the way back . . . and Joe Stalin being a realistic cuss was more interested in knowing what Churchill said to Roosevelt . . . than what was said when they were all three together. I don't blame him. . . . I would be the same way on a three man conference. On a three man conference, one an atheist and two of them Christians. One a Communist, two of them capitalists. One a dictator, two of them elected representatives of a free people. One can talk only his native language of Russian, the other two can confer together.
>
> We don't make progress in a conference like that. . . . Stalin feels that he is being taken for a ride. Let's meet them once man to man as equals across the table . . . say, "Joe . . . you have a great country over there. . . . We want to be friends with you . . . we need your help on certain matters. . . . Joe . . . we are going to let you write the ticket for the dealings between Russia and the United States. . . . If you think it is a good idea to have newspapers and visitors from your country visit ours, that will be all right; that is, provided that we can have the same. . . ."[8]

---

[7] They were made obvious in the famous October 1944 "Percentage Agreements" between Churchill and Stalin. See Winston S. Churchill, *The Second World War: Triumph and Tragedy,* vol. 6 (Cambridge, Mass.: Houghton-Mifflin Co., 1953), pp. 227-28.

[8] *Vital Speeches,* vol. 12, no. 17 (June 15, 1946), p. 251.

Mundt went on to assert that if the United States would let the Russians know that it was not afraid of them and would cut out appeasement, things would work out. He continued, "God has been good to the United States. . . . I am convinced that only stupidity or cupidity on our part can so mismanage our foreign and domestic affairs that a war with Russia would become inevitable." A realistic policy, said Mundt, "will reject appeasement of Russia and renounce opposition to Russia in the same breath. . . ." [9]

The important point—and it becomes quite clear in the statement by Mr. Mundt—is that American attitudes toward the developing postwar situation were, on the whole, quite abstract. Whatever the particular determinants of specific actions, the terms in which they were interpreted by Americans were remote from the actual choices that face decision makers in historic circumstances. The mediation which, according to Hegel, bridges the abstract and the particular was absent from American understanding of the international political process.[10] We did not ask whether an independent Poland could be both democratic and friendly to the Soviet Union. We did not ask what risks the Soviet leaders perceived or how they understood their responses to these perceptions. Those few among our important figures, such as Henry Wallace, who, realistically or not, did ask these questions about the Soviet Union failed in their turn to understand American choices pragmatically. They failed to ask what risks would be run by the United States or by the nations of western Europe if their analyses were incorrect. They failed to weigh the possibility that the Soviet Union might define its security needs even more broadly in the face of weakness or political instability in Europe. And they did not ask whether Soviet hegemony in Europe was consistent with the interests of the United States or with the values for which the war had been fought.

Negative Western interpretations of Soviet motives were shaped by the brutal Soviet behavior in eastern Europe, Soviet reluctance to withdraw from Iran, Soviet demands upon Turkey, the Greek civil war, huge Soviet industrial withdrawals from Germany, organization of the Cominform, the coup in Czechoslovakia, the Berlin blockade, and eventually, the Korean War, although that occurred after the initial organization of NATO. At last a consistent pattern was perceived, and

---

[9] Ibid.

[10] See Henry Kissinger's introduction to his book, *The Troubled Partnership* (New York: McGraw-Hill Book Co., 1965), p. 24, for a similar viewpoint.

it was a frightening pattern. In the winter of 1948, as the Forrestal diaries reveal, top-level intelligence analyses in the United States optimistically projected that the Soviet Union would not attack for at least the next six months.[11]

A Possible Soviet View

Yet the situation might have looked equally bad from a Soviet point of view. The Italian settlement, the protests over eastern Europe, and the abrupt ending of Lend-Lease might have appeared as hostile acts. Anglo-American bizonal fusion in Germany and the increases in the level of permitted production in the western zones, although legitimate responses to administrative difficulties, could have been viewed in the Soviet Union as indications of increasing Western hostility and as evidence of an intention to use Germany against the East. The failure of the Moscow meeting of foreign ministers in March-April 1947, the Truman Doctrine response to the Greek civil war (more reluctantly supported by Stalin than the West realized), French adherence to the Anglo-American program for Germany, and the veto of the Soviet proposal for four-power control of the Ruhr must have appeared as sledgehammer blows to the Kremlin. This impression may have been reinforced critically in the summer of 1947 when JCS 1067, providing for the dismantling of German heavy industry, was formally revoked. The political exigencies confronting the Soviet Union after its rejection of the Marshall Plan, the forced industrialization of eastern Europe, which likely was necessary for Soviet security reasons, the difficulties arising within the satellite nations as a consequence of the consolidation of political control, and the valid fear that the Communists would lose the election in a Czechoslovakia that had strong historic ties to the West created enormous practical difficulties for the men in the Kremlin.

A Scholarly Reassessment

Let us see if we can analyze the situation in Europe independently of the normal cold war or revisionist interpretations. At the close of the Second World War, the Axis had been defeated and was occupied by the victorious powers. As a consequence, there was an enormous power

[11] James Forrestal, *The Forrestal Diaries,* ed. Walter Millis (New York: The Viking Press, 1951), pp. 387 and 391.

8

vacuum in the center of Europe. England and France were economically devastated. Large Communist parties existed in France and Italy and participated in the government until the advent of the Marshall Plan. The Soviet Union had become the master of eastern Germany and much of eastern Europe—a major route through which attacks upon it had been launched in the past. To use a slang phrase, Europe was up for grabs. Almost everything was in flux. Uncertainty was the keynote. Almost any major political or military action might have set in motion enormous and unpredictable change.

The Soviet Union could not know where democratic political processes would lead in east Europe, although it no doubt knew that they would not lead in a pro-Soviet direction, except perhaps in Bulgaria. The United States could not rule out Communist revolutions in Italy and France. Nor, with Soviet consolidation of east Europe, could the United States rule out what many fear today: the Finlandization of west Europe. Indeed, the absence of strong political structures in west Europe might have tempted Russian pressure, if only to prevent manifestly anti-Soviet developments.

The conspiratorial theories that each side held at the time may have been functional in some genuine sense. The gentlemanly bargaining and absence of suspicion that some historians argue would have avoided the cold war might have been even more detrimental to world peace than those at least partly misguided views that produced the cold war. The postwar situation was fraught with uncertainty and danger for both the Soviet Union and the United States. The failure by timely intervention to organize two blocs might have led to situations that could have confirmed the most extreme conspiratorial fears and might have produced the catastrophy of a new world war. If the natural process of events had produced a major political shift in Europe tending to thrust it entirely into one of the two camps, or so much uncertainty and instability that major military intervention seemed required for security reasons, disaster would likely have resulted. Thus, there was a real danger. Moreover, even if the view that the Soviet Union was *actively* seeking the military conquest of Europe was wrong, it should be remembered that the Soviet Union had never been reluctant to use its muscle to support its policies. Its brutal policies in eastern Europe, even if understandable in security terms, hardly showed respect for the independence of other nations. Security needs can be interpreted quite broadly if the opportunity is available.

9

The Official Response to the Situation

High officials in the West felt it was extremely important to organize security organizations designed to thwart Soviet pressures. At the beginning of 1948, after discussions with the American secretary of state, the British foreign minister, Ernest Bevin, proposed an alliance of Great Britain, France, Belgium, the Netherlands, and Luxembourg based upon the "conception of the unity of Europe and the preservation of Europe as the heart of Western civilization." [12] Bevin proposed that the Anglo-French Treaty of Dunkirk, which had been signed in March 1947, become the nucleus of a larger alliance that might be extended in time to include "other historic members of European civilization." [13] This quickly resulted in the Brussels Pact of March 1948, a 50-year treaty of economic, social, and cultural collaboration and of collective self-defense. The speed with which the proposal was adopted by the various European powers is a striking indication of how serious the international situation seemed to a majority of Europeans.

Article IV of the Brussels Pact provided that "if any of the High Contracting Parties should be the object of an armed attack in Europe, the other High Contracting Parties will, in accordance with Article 51 of the Charter of the United Nations, afford the party so attacked all the military and other aid and assistance in their power." [14] Within a month a permanent consultative organization had been established, including a Council, a Permanent Commission, and a Permanent Military Commission. From the very beginning American and Canadian military observers were associated with the work of the Military Commission. President Truman told Congress that the significance of this new organization "goes far beyond the actual terms of the agreement itself. It is a notable step in the direction of unity in Europe. . . . this development deserves our full support. I am confident that the United States will, by the appropriate means, extend to the free nations the support which the situation requires." [15]

These developments were going on while the Marshall Plan was still being debated by Congress. During this debate President Truman

---

[12] Hansard, *Parliamentary Debates,* 446 H.C. DEB 5 S Col. 396-97 (January 22, 1948).

[13] Reitzel, Kaplan, and Coblenz, *U.S. Foreign Policy,* p. 124.

[14] Ibid.

[15] U.S. Department of State, *Bulletin,* vol. 18 (March 28, 1948), p. 419.

called a high level conference to consider the military situation in Europe within the context of the Marshall Plan debate. He was advised that western European fears of Communist uprisings or pressures from the Soviet Union would interfere seriously with economic recovery. According to John Foster Dulles, then a consultant to the State Department, only a decisive move by the United States would check the fear inspired by Moscow. The President therefore agreed to proceed along the lines of a North Atlantic regional pact.[16]

Arthur Vandenberg, who was present as representative of non-isolationist Republicans in the Senate, stated that the Senate liked the idea of regional associations and was likely to approve the development of such associations for purposes of collective defense.[17] Senator Vandenberg consequently introduced a resolution, which was passed on 11 June 1948, that encouraged the President to proceed to the "progressive development of regional and other collective arrangements for individual and collective self-defense in accordance with the purposes, principles, and provisions of the Charter"[18] of the United Nations. This was the first occasion on which the Congress encouraged an American military alliance during time of peace.

The executive branch acted swiftly. In July 1948, exploratory talks with the members of the Brussels Pact about a regional military arrangement for the North Atlantic area began in Canada. Denmark, Norway, and Portugal soon joined the talks, increasing the number of parties to twelve.

The agreement establishing NATO was signed by the President on 4 April 1949 and ratified by the Senate in late July 1949. Despite the strength of the support from west Europe and within the American foreign policy community, the debate in the Senate indicated strong popular doubts about the treaty commitments. However, reservations against stationing American troops in Europe, against recognizing a moral or legal obligation to furnish or supply arms, armaments, naval or air supplies, including atomic weapons and information, were defeated.

Many important segments of public opinion led by such individuals as Eleanor Roosevelt, Max Lerner, the influential Democratic Representative Sabath of Illinois, and Representative Ellis Patterson were disturbed by the implication that American policy was moving away

---

16 Reitzel, Kaplan, and Coblenz, *U.S. Foreign Policy,* p. 125.
17 John Foster Dulles, *War or Peace* (New York: Macmillan Co., 1950), pp. 95-96.
18 *Congressional Record,* vol. 94, pt. 6, 80th Congress, 2d session, p. 7791.

11

from support of the United Nations in favor of a military coalition against the Soviet Union. For this reason, the treaty included an attempt to establish a relationship to the United Nations Charter. Article 5 of the treaty, which set forth the primary obligation, stated that:

> The Parties agree that an armed attack against one or more of them in Europe or in North America shall be considered an attack against them all; and consequently they agree that, if such an armed attack occurs, each of them, in exercise of individual or collective self-defense recognized by Article 51 of the Charter of the United Nations, will assist the Party or Parties so attacked by taking forthwith, individually and in concert with the other Parties, such action as it deems necessary, including the use of armed force, to restore and maintain the security of the North Atlantic area.[19]

Article 51 of the charter did establish the right of members individually or collectively to take measures of self-defense. However, an effort was also made to relate NATO to Article 52, which refers to regional organizations. Depending upon one's view of this matter, this attempt can be viewed either as a violation of the charter or as a creative application of it, for the regional organizations to which Article 52 was supposed to refer were intended to deal with breaches of the peace *within* regions and not to establish alliances against extraregional powers. On the other hand, in fairness, it must be noted that the original assumption underlying an effective United Nations—the harmonious interests of the victorious major powers—had already broken down and, thus, required some substitute if the organization was to function effectively. Yet, was the NATO organization genuinely intended to operate through the United Nations? This seems dubious; in this sense, the critics of NATO were right in their judgment of its implications, if not in their assessment of the requirements of the situation.

The NATO treaty established a North Atlantic Council, which met for the first time in Washington in September 1949. This executive organization established a Defense Committee, on which the chiefs of staff of each of the treaty powers sat, and a Standing Group, with representatives from the United States, Great Britain, and France, that was intended to provide continuing guidance for five regional military groups. The Defense Committee established a Military and Supply Board to organize industrial mobilization in western Europe and, later,

---

[19] For text of the North Atlantic Treaty, see *United Nations Treaty Series,* vol. 34, no. 541 (1949), pp. 244-55.

a Defense Financial and Economic Committee. By January 1950, it approved recommendations for an integrated defense plan for the entire North Atlantic area. The United States quickly established the need for, and later implemented, a Defense Assistance Pact. However, despite these impressive American commitments to Europe, neither an effective command structure nor an adequate defense base in Europe was established.

In 1948 the great debate in the Defense Department had been over whether, if the Russians attacked, American forces in Europe could be withdrawn successfully or whether they would be captured. The situation in 1950 was not much better. Few would have argued that a viable west European military establishment existed. On the other hand, the organization of NATO presumably provided the psychological lift necessary to sustain an environment for economic recovery that was essential for rebuilding a strong west Europe. It also established a long-term American commitment to European unity and in part led to the pressure within the United States for German rearmament as one aspect of a reasonable defense posture for west Europe.[20]

---

[20] See Dean Acheson, *Present at the Creation: My Years at the State Department* (New York: W. W. Norton and Co., 1969), pp. 508, 552, 565-71, 573-77, and 628-31. See also the discussion of NSC-68, pp. 454, 486-97, 546 and 604.

2

The Early History of NATO

The German and the French Questions

Because the German and French questions are so important to a clear understanding of the present situation of NATO, their history will be given in modest detail. From the vantage point of 1972 it is difficult to remember the extraordinary passions that invested the question of German rearmament shortly after the close of the Second World War or the frustrations of the French that resulted from American dominance. Yet, raising the question of German rearmament led to the proposal for a European Defense Community; and the resistance to that proposal resulted in an actually independent German military contribution to NATO, but only after the most agonizing of appraisals. Although German rearmament was advocated by some American officials before the outbreak of hostilities in Korea, the compelling reasons for American support for that decision were connected organically to that event, and illustrate the global interlocking of foreign problems.[1]

The importance of West Germany in west European defense preparations had long been recognized. Without German terrain, the strategic plans of the NATO command would lack sufficient depth for defensive maneuvers. But the use of German territory did not require the use of German soldiers. Although General Lucius Clay advocated the

---

[1] Because of the great importance of the events leading to German rearmament in helping to shape the perspectives of the participants, they are reconstructed here in a way that provides some flavor of the pressure placed on the French. Unfortunately, the author's original citations are lost, although they come from the *New York Times* and the *Washington Post,* and only the unfootnoted reconstructions are left. They are, however, quite accurate in substance, although other historians might interpret them differently.

15

use of German troops before Korea,[2] the British military took a more cautious view: that whether Germany should be rearmed was a matter for the statesman but that, if instructed, they could do an effective job of it.

The French military were aware that the Soviet Union had an estimated 150 divisions on an active footing, although because of defense needs elsewhere, the Soviet Union would not be able to employ more than 80 divisions in an attack upon the West. Thus, a Soviet attack could be repelled by a defense force of 60-80 divisions provided that half of these were armored. A force of that magnitude was beyond the existing capabilities of the West. However, despite the fact that this would require a German contribution, the French were still unwilling to face up to it.

Because of the strength of the early opposition to German rearmament, American Secretary of State Dean Acheson insisted that American policy had not undergone any change with respect to the arming of West Germany, and stressed continued official opposition to such a course. On 20 December 1949 the West German government, understandably worried about the defense problem, asked the British, French, and American allied High Commissioners to inform it officially what plans, if any, were being made by the North Atlantic pact powers to defend Germany in the event of war with the Soviet Union.[3] The Bonn regime expressed fear that only a holding operation would be made on the Elbe, and that a serious western effort would not be made short of the Rhine. The Bonn government, however, did not indicate any desire to rearm in order to defend its own territory.

In March 1950 General Billotte, who had recently resigned as French representative on the Military Committee of the United Nations, said that in the event of war with the Soviet Union NATO should fight as far as possible to the east. He said this could not be done without a certain rearmament of Germany—but France and the other signatories of the Atlantic pact must be provided for first. However, his statement was at odds with official French thinking. The same month British opposition leader Winston Churchill stated in Parliament that the effective defense of European frontiers could not be achieved if the

---

[2] The Joint Chiefs of Staff endorsed a plan for German divisions in the autumn of 1949. James L. Richardson, *Germany and the Atlantic Alliance: The Interaction of Strategy and Politics* (Cambridge: Harvard University Press, 1966), p. 18.

[3] Acheson, *Present at the Creation,* p. 444.

German contribution were excluded from the thoughts of those who were responsible.

Nevertheless, because of French sensitivities, at a meeting of the chiefs of staff of the NATO powers in March 1950 N. E. Halaby, assistant for military affairs to Secretary of Defense Louis Johnson, said that any initiative for the discussion of the German problem must come from the nations bordering Germany. It was understood that the chiefs had agreed tacitly not to discuss the German problem, and that, if the defense ministers did discuss the issue, the discussions would be only informal. Mr. Johnson later implied that the issue never arose at the meeting.

Early in April, Secretary of State Acheson temporized. He said that the American position on the rearming of Germany and the dismantling of German plants was unchanged. He did express the hope that the Federal Republic would accept the invitation to become a member of the Council of Europe.

Shortly before the May 1950 meetings of the three powers and the Atlantic treaty powers, Acheson, when asked whether it was true that proposals for the inclusion of Germany in the political and economic machinery of NATO were being studied, gave a "diplomatic" response. He said all kinds of ideas were being studied. French sources emphasized that if Germany were brought within the Atlantic Council, she must not be included within the military framework of NATO. France feared in addition that a European organization not including Britain would be dominated by Germany.

Meanwhile pressure from Washington for the integration of West Germany with other west European countries—short of the rearmament of Germany—was increasing. On 2 May 1950 State Department official Francis H. Russell stated that the North Atlantic foreign ministers who were to meet in London knew that Germany could not be kept weak and in quarantine without gravely impairing the health and strength of all western Europe. They also knew, he said, that Germany's neighbors were too close to the painful past to be able to view with calm the prospect of uncontrolled and renewed German strength. Russell pointed out that they were faced, more urgently than ever, with the task of making plans to foster the growth of true democracy in Germany and progressively taking the free German peoples into partnership.

However, at the meeting of the Atlantic powers, the foreign ministers agreed to postpone the discussion of Germany. It was felt

17

that, if German rearmament were desired, it would be better to invite Germany to join a strong functioning organization at a time when selective use of the German potential could be made by that organization.[4] Early in June, General Omar Bradley expressed the view that West Germany was strongly anti-Soviet and said that he regarded this as a source of strength for the democratic nations of the West in their dealings with the Soviet Union. However, he refused to discuss a recent request from the Bonn government for a police force on the ground that the subject was political.

In late July 1950, just prior to the first meetings of the North Atlantic Council deputies but after the outbreak of the Korean War, a French spokesman, referring to reports that the United States would like to discuss the subject of German rearmament, stated that he did not see how the subject could be placed on the agenda. He said that the position of France had not changed either with respect to the impossibility of reconstituting, in any form whatsoever, a German army or with respect to the necessity of maintaining international control of the Ruhr and the limitations and interdictions imposed on heavy German industry.[5]

An American briefing officer outlined the assumptions underlying American strategic reasoning during the preparatory conferences before the formal meetings of the North Atlantic Council. He stated that, when the foreign ministers of the Atlantic Pact powers had met in May, it was assumed that NATO would have at least five years to organize its defenses against a Communist assault, and that the Soviet Union and its satellites would not attack until they thought themselves fully prepared to gain an assured victory. He said that assumption had been negated by the attack of the North Korean forces. Korea had convinced Western strategists that aggression could be expected at any time.[6]

On 25 July, under pressure, French spokesmen indicated a tactical retreat from the earlier French position that German industry must not be permitted to manufacture materials of war. They proposed that Germany manufacture arms that would be used by the North Atlantic powers to defend the West.[7] It seems German arms were less sensitive to the French than German soldiers.

---

[4] Ibid., pp. 514-15.

[5] Reitzel, Kaplan, and Coblenz, *U.S. Foreign Policy,* p. 288.

[6] Ibid., p. 289.

[7] Acheson, *Present at the Creation,* p. 565ff.

Meanwhile an anonymous American spokesman implied the inadequacy of the French reconsideration. He pointed out that the real job facing the council was to raise 36 divisions by 1952, or 1953 at the latest, to defend western Europe. The Korean fighting, he said, had emphasized the importance of ground troops. Europe's defense could no longer be viewed as a question of American dollars and increased arms production in Europe. Manpower was the crucial item. The critical defense area was West Germany. The Western allies, he said, had only seven understrength divisions facing an estimated 200,000 Russian-armed-and-trained East German "policemen" backed by a potential Russian strength of 175 combat divisions. Larger forces were needed in West Germany to guard against a German "civil war." France was tied down in Indochina, but might increase her European strength from five to 20 divisions. The Scandinavian countries might provide a small number of divisions. But the 40 million people in West Germany might some day provide up to 25 divisions for European defense. He noted, however, that there were still no plans to use that manpower in the foreseeable future.

Meanwhile in response to domestic murmurings, Jules Moch, the French defense minister, was telling his National Assembly that there could be no question of a French infantry, British navy, and American air force to defend Europe. France expected Britain and the United States also to make ground force commitments to the defense of Europe. Nevertheless, by early August France indicated her resolution by promising to equip 15 divisions, with American aid, as her share of the Western rearmament program. It was pointed out that this effort would not have been possible except for the firmness that America was showing in Korea and the confidence this created in France concerning the intentions of the United States.

However, the effort did not appear sufficient to John Sherman Cooper of the American delegation, who warned that European plans for rearmament were cautious and inadequate. On 11 August the Consultative Assembly of the Council of Europe recommended the creation of a European army on a motion by Winston Churchill, thus introducing a novel element into proposals for Western defense. On 15 August an American spokesman gave qualified approval to French rearmament suggestions. He noted, however, that France's raising of 15 divisions was contingent upon the stationing of five divisions apiece in Europe by Great Britain and the United States. He pointed out that the United States could not promise to divert that much manpower to the continent of Europe, given the limited size of the American army, at the same time that it was fighting in Korea.

On 19 August John Sherman Cooper said that the United States must show its firm intention to take part in the defense of Europe in the initial stage of an assault, should one occur. This meant, he said, that the United States and Great Britain had to commit men and equipment before such an assault began. Although he did not make any recommendations for the rearming of Germany, he did state that it was inevitable and moral that Germany be given the opportunity to defend herself.

Thus, the United States felt that it had to commit its ground forces to Europe for a successful defense and for morale purposes, although she was short of troops in Korea. The price for this would be German armed forces; these were essential, in the American view, for a successful ground defense. The U.S., therefore, began to hint that its commitment to European defense was contingent upon European acceptance of a German contribution. This was the beginning of the agonizing bargaining process that led to the commitment of five American divisions to Europe and the appointment of an American general as Supreme Allied Commander Europe in return for French acceptance of a German manpower contribution.

Meanwhile, an American spokesman in West Germany stated flatly that Germany would play a role in the defense plans of the West and added that the Germans would take part in the decisions concerning their role. He also stated that the three Western Allied High Commissioners were studying the proposal of Chancellor Konrad Adenauer that a West German force, equal in size, training, and equipment to that of the Soviet zone police force, be created. Adenauer, however, was opposed to a German army, except perhaps as part of a European army. In Germany the Social Democratic party leaders attacked the Adenauer proposal for armed police. On 6 September Secretary of State Acheson said that it was important to find an appropriate way in which Germany could contribute to the defense of Europe.

The United States then took steps related to its bargaining with France. On 9 September President Truman approved "substantial" increases in American forces in Europe in the "sincere expectation" that other North Atlantic Treaty powers would "keep in step." [8] It was

---

[8] Acheson, *Present at the Creation,* pp. 439-40.

20

reported from London that this step would encourage the west European governments that had been anxious as a result of American reverses in Korea and that had wondered what would happen if the East Germans embarked upon a war of aggression against West Germany. Senator Henry Cabot Lodge spoke of a plan to raise and equip 30 American divisions, 20 of which would be stationed in Europe.[9]

The issue was still to go through many twists and turns. The New York meeting of the foreign ministers agreed that a German national army was not an objective. This was not sufficiently reassuring to the French foreign minister, Robert Schuman. Jules Moch flew over to the NATO meetings to support Foreign Minister Schuman. He stated that France would agree to a larger role for a West German police force but that it would not agree to the creation of German divisions. The United States tried to secure agreement in principle to the future creation of West German divisions but met opposition.

On 19 September, to reassure an increasingly disturbed West Germany, the foreign ministers of Great Britain, France, and the United States declared that their occupation forces in Germany were also security forces for the defense of the free world and that they would treat any attack against the Federal Republic or Berlin as an attack upon themselves.[10]

However, as the Atlantic Council recessed, reports circulated that Ernest Bevin had received instructions to support in principle the arming of West Germany. The United States pressed this issue again on 23 September in a meeting of the Big Three foreign ministers. The U.S. claimed that the rising volume of Western arms production could be absorbed only if West German units were created. American spokesmen emphasized for their French listeners that these forces would not be under the control of the Bonn government and would take orders only from the unified command. On 25 September there was an agreement in principle that Germany "should be enabled to contribute to the build-up of the defense of Western Europe" and a statement that the manner in which the contribution would be made was undergoing study.[11]

---

[9] For Lodge's general role in this debate, see ibid., p. 638. But the British and French argued for German financial support rather than for an adequate troop contingent.

[10] Ibid., pp. 714-15.

[11] Ibid., p. 444.

The French continued to object to American pressure and argued strongly that only on the basis of French leadership and a Franco-German understanding could the issue be settled in a manner consistent with European unity. The French reasonably argued that the Schuman plan to pool western Europe's coal and steel resources should be permitted to establish the framework of unity before the armament program for Germany was pushed. The French evidently refrained from stating the obvious: If the American timetable for a Soviet attack was accurate, its plans for German rearmament would not be effectuated until years after Europe had been lost. The French did accuse the U.S. of delaying efforts to achieve the defense of Europe, of jeopardizing final agreement on the Schuman plan, of upsetting relations between France and Germany, and of arousing suspicion in pro-American French circles where none had previously existed.

On 19 October it was reported in Paris that Foreign Minister Robert Schuman would propose to the French cabinet that the question of German rearmament be solved by merging the continental European forces into a single army and unifying the armament production of the western part of the continent. Such a plan was proposed on 24 October by Premier Pleven.[12] However, Pleven opposed German units of a size acceptable to the United States.

The United States responded with heavy-handed pressure. It was reliably reported that if the government of Premier Pleven would not permit an appropriate German role in European defense another French government might. The United States was understood to have sent a "stiff" note to the French explaining that small German units would be useless. It was stated privately that if the French were "realistic," they would recognize that their defense efforts were completely dependent upon American aid.

Chancellor Adenauer stated that West Germany would make an adequate contribution to the defense of Western Europe if it enjoyed equal rights and was part of a coalition sufficiently strong to deter Soviet aggression. He thus indicated an unwillingness to provoke the Soviet Union by arming Germany until the West was strong enough to discourage Soviet aggression. He remained opposed to an independent German army.[13] The United States, meanwhile, was refusing

---

[12] Ibid., p. 458.

[13] See Richardson, *Germany and the Atlantic Alliance,* p. 21, for the debate between the CDU and the SPD on this issue.

to name a commander for the unified forces or to commit additional American forces to Europe until France changed its position on the German question.

Chinese intervention in the Korean War modified the attitude of Paris. The French feared that the United States might neglect Europe for its concerns in the Pacific. Therefore, the French accepted a proposal for German combat teams the size of a third of a division.[14]

This story need not be continued in detail. These plans eventually collapsed with French defeat of the proposed European Defense Community in 1954, despite enormous American pressure, and paradoxically resulted in the Eden plan that effectively established an independent German army as part of the NATO forces. The Soviet thrust which these forces were designed to oppose never occurred and could not have been halted by them had it occurred. On the other hand, despite the possible damage to European unity and the alienation of the French, the favorable psychological impact of the American commitment upon European politics was enormous. Under this mantle of American reassurance, despite numerous Berlin crises and nuclear blackmailing by Khrushchev, Europe was able to forge forward economically, becoming the vigorous entity it is today. It was also under this mantle of American armed might that Europe acquired the self-confidence necessary to pursue independent political policies.

Yet, even if Americans forgot the nature of their pressure, the French never forgot. Eventually another issue—the nuclear issue—was to plague NATO. American insensitivity on this issue was to do enormous damage to the organization.

Transition: The Nuclear Question

In the mid-1950s, beneath the surface of stability—loose bipolarity[15]— a number of symptoms prefiguring grave difficulties for NATO were becoming apparent. French political democracy was on the road to decline under the impact of a number of politically unsuccessful colonial wars. The United States was on the verge of the misleading missile-gap controversy, which heralded a decline in the credibility of the American deterrent in the defense of west Europe.

---

[14] Acheson, *Present at the Creation,* p. 747ff.

[15] See Morton A. Kaplan, *System and Process in International Politics* (New York: John Wiley & Sons, 1957), for a definition of loose bipolarity.

The 1957 launch of the first Sputnik dramatized a factor of major strategic importance: the vulnerability of the continental United States to Soviet nuclear weaponry. It became clear to all that the United States no longer could employ its strategic nuclear force against the Soviet Union in response to an attack upon Western Europe without risking nuclear damage to itself. Although President John F. Kennedy might later evoke an enthusiastic response by proclaiming in Berlin, "Ich bin ein Berliner," his listeners were fully aware that he was *not* a Berliner. Nor was he a Parisian or a Londoner. America might—and so thought many, should—risk much for Western Europe, but few Americans saw their interests as identical to those of their European allies in the ultimate crisis. Therefore, our NATO allies concluded that they could not depend upon the United States to protect their interests in the same way in which it would protect its own. Conceivably, they might even come under pressure from the United States, as in 1938 Czechoslovakia came under pressure from Britain and France, to make concessions to an external foe to avoid the danger of world war.

The French, who earlier had been bludgeoned by the United States into acceptance of German rearmament, were most alert to this problem.[16] After returning to the presidency of France, General de Gaulle asked the United States to establish within NATO a triumvirate of Britain, France, and the United States to consult on the use of the American nuclear deterrent during war in western Europe. This proposal was turned down under the Eisenhower administration, and France withdrew more deeply into dependence on its own unilateral nuclear force. These events played a role in leading General de Gaulle to the decisions that later withdrew France from NATO's joint command systems. Without effectively interfering with French pursuit of an independent nuclear path, the United States nonetheless irritated the French considerably by placing in their path minor obstacles, such as the refusal to permit the French to import from the United States the computers needed for their nuclear program.

In recognition of this problem as a major threat to the cohesion of NATO, this writer proposed a joint NATO nuclear force that would be employed under either of two conditions: Soviet first use of nuclear weapons against west Europe or a large-scale Soviet invasion of west

---

[16] See, for example, Raymond Aron, *The Great Debate: Theories of Nuclear Strategy* (New York: Doubleday and Co., 1965).

Europe that it would not halt upon demand.[17] This joint NATO nuclear force would have operated without an American veto. A modified version of this proposal retaining the American veto, and based upon Polaris submarines, was adopted by the Eisenhower administration.

After John F. Kennedy assumed the presidency, this emaciated version of the proposal for a joint NATO force was further weakened. The Polaris submarines were to be replaced by surface ships, easily vulnerable to Soviet attack, and each ship was to be manned by crews from six different allied nations. Each of the six nations would have a veto on use of the force. Only the Germans appeared to go along with it, presumably because they were so dependent upon American protection. Although this force was supported by some in the Kennedy administration as a potential step toward a genuinely joint force, others mistakenly saw it as a painless method for halting the French drive toward a unilateral force. The perceived insult to French suscepti-bilities was further compounded by the Skybolt decisions reached by President Kennedy and Prime Minister Macmillan. Although the deci-sion on Skybolt was technically sound, and the associated decisions merely awkwardly stage-managed, the Gaullist perception of an Anglo-American special partnership and of a return to the imperial American methods of the late 1940s was not entirely inaccurate.

This was also the period in which the McNamara Defense Depart-ment was adopting the pause strategy for NATO. In this instance, the United States was caught between the requirements of sound defense policy and the message being communicated to its NATO allies by the implementation of that policy. If a war began in central Europe, it was obviously advisable to attempt to contain it without resorting to large-scale use of nuclear weapons. However, the American pressure for adoption of the strategy was interpreted by many Europeans as confirmation of the reluctance of the United States to use nuclear weapons in Europe's defense.

Most West European leaders did not want to think about fighting a war in Europe; they wanted only to deter it. In their view, the most credible deterrent was an automatic one. In the American view, credi-bility would be diminished if the actual use was highly implausible. Supposedly automatic deterrence systems function well if there is no crisis, that is, if they are not tested. In a crisis, however, fears concerning

---

[17] "Problems of Coalition and Deterrence," in Klaus Knorr, ed., *NATO and American Security* (Princeton: Princeton University Press, 1959), pp. 127-50.

automatic deterrence systems are likely soon to be communicated to would-be aggressors. This soon becomes apparent to those who, charged with actual responsibility, think deeply about the actual use of nuclear systems.

Perhaps this point could have been made successfully to the Europeans if the United States had been willing to relinquish some of its decision-making control over the use of nuclear weapons. However, with respect to the use of its nuclear weapons, the United States demanded complete and implicit trust—a form of faith that often breaks down in far more intimate relationships than those that existed between the United States and its NATO allies.

Crisis and Détente

The years following 1960 saw a number of parallel but interlocking developments that seemed to herald a highly successful world role for the United States. In the fall of 1962 President Kennedy stood down Premier Khrushchev during the Cuban missile controversy.[18] During the same years the Kennedy administration pursued a rapid buildup of the American strategic arsenal, including both the Minuteman system and the Polaris submarine fleet. By 1965 American strategic nuclear superiority was so enormous that Secretary of Defense McNamara called a halt to the buildup and confidently predicted that the Soviet nuclear forces would level off before reaching numerical parity with the United States, a position he consistently continued to maintain in the 1966 and 1967 Congressional hearings.[19]

Détente with the Soviet Union was confidently pursued, beginning with the nuclear test ban. The recurrent Berlin crises became a matter of past history. General de Gaulle's policies were based on a belief that the United States was so preeminently the world's most powerful state that, in order to maintain some kind of world balance, France had to lean somewhat toward the Soviet Union which, he was confident, had

[18] For a somewhat different view, see Graham Allison, "Cuban Missiles and Kennedy Macho: New Evidence to Dispel the Myth," *Washington Monthly,* October 1972, pp. 14-19.

[19] See statement of Secretary of Defense Robert S. McNamara before the House Subcommittee on Defense Appropriations for fiscal years 1967-71, "Defense Program and 1967 Defense Budget" (mimeographed, February 23, 1966), p. 41, for a full statement of the McNamara position. Also see an analysis of that statement in William R. Kintner, *Peace and the Strategy Conflict* (New York: Praeger Publishers, Inc., 1967), pp. 253-60.

no aggressive designs against Western Europe, at least as long as the United States remained powerful.

In the first half of the decade, American involvement in Vietnam was relatively noncontroversial and relatively insignificant in terms of the commitment of American resources and its impact on the American dollar balance. Secretary of State Dean Rusk was confidently asserting the success of the policies that had brought the United States from the troubled and tension-ridden 1950s to a stable 1960s, in which American policies had achieved worldwide success.

The one apparent trouble area was the conventional balance in west Europe, where the NATO powers had never achieved the force-level goals that had been called for at various NATO meetings. However, Alain Enthoven of the Defense Department argued that the apparent Russian superiority was very misleading. The Soviet Union had a large advantage in numbers of divisions, but the American army division with its supporting personnel ran over 40,000 men while the Russian division with its supporting personnel bulked somewhere in the neighborhood of 18,000 men. According to this interpretation the Russians would be unable to achieve the three-to-one advantage that the offense required over defense in order to launch an attack. Moreover, he contended that although Russia had more planes and tanks, the Western planes were better and NATO had more antitank weapons.[20]

As with many of the arguments emanating from the Office of the Secretary of Defense in the days of McNamara, these arguments were based upon mirror-imaging. The Russians were assumed to have the same strategic objectives as the United States and were therefore assumed to have made stupid decisions. In the strategic field, it was assumed that the Russians must be ignorant of the formula governing area of destruction and warhead size, thus accounting for their procurement of large nuclear delivery systems—an inefficient method of attacking undefended cities. If, contrary to the assumption of the Department of Defense, the Russians wished to maintain some potential for a war-fighting capability and to secure natural hardening advantages against defensive interception, the Russian procurement decisions may have made sense. If Russian conventional attack plans were similar to American, calling for long-term supply capabilities and individual manpower replacements, the Enthoven thesis on the conventional balance

---

[20] See Alain Enthoven, "Arms and Men: The Military Balance in Europe, " *Interplay,* May 1969.

27

might have been reasonable. If, on the other hand, the Russian divisions were designed, as they clearly appear to be, for shock tactics in a rapid war of movement—with rapid replacement of entire units—then the smaller Russian division would encompass more fighting potential than the larger American division. It would do the United States little good to be in a preferred position for a long war if it lost the short war. In their weapons procurement policy, the Russians optimized for the European theater. The United States procured extremely expensive weapons systems for Europe which would work under all kinds of extreme conditions, but which were not optimized on a cost-effective basis for the conditions existing in Europe.

The Decline

After 1965 the American world position worsened. The inconclusive character of the Vietnamese war accelerated this process. The cost of fighting the war interfered seriously with the design and procurement of modernized weapons systems. The Soviet Union began to catch up with, and eventually surpassed, the United States in numbers of strategic nuclear weapons. The strains upon the federal budget soon produced pressures for a reduction in American commitments. Inflation produced a balance-of-payments crisis. The unpopularity of the Vietnamese war complicated alliance diplomacy throughout the world.

The fall of 1968 saw the brutal suppression of Czechoslovak liberalism by invading troops of the Warsaw Treaty Organization (WTO). This caused at least a momentary intense shock throughout the world and a reassessment of Soviet motivations. Moreover, that invasion revealed the competence with which the Soviet Union could mobilize pact forces in a swift and effective military movement. During the same period the informed public was slowly becoming aware that McNamara's projections of Soviet strategic weapons acquisitions had been consistently wrong since 1965.

One other heavy blow occurred at the same time: the notice of French withdrawal from the integrated NATO command, which entailed the removal of American military facilities from France, the severe reduction in dependable NATO port facilities in Europe, and the reduction in assured military space. After de Gaulle's retirement, these latter factors were modified somewhat by the Pompidou regime. The French fleet in the Mediterranean became more cooperative in maneuvers, overflight facilities were more dependable, and military communications improved. Even so, for military planning purposes, the situation was far removed from the days when France had been integrated into the NATO command structure. In addition, these improvements were perhaps more than offset by substantial buildups in Soviet manpower and equipment.

The events in Europe were to some extent compensated for by tensions on the Sino-Soviet border. Hints of a nuclear strike against China began to emanate from the Soviet Union in 1968. Eventually Soviet forces on the Sino-Soviet border were built up to a strength of over a million men. Yet that buildup did not interfere with Soviet force postures in Europe, where substantial increases also occurred during the period 1968-1973.

3
The Nixon Era

The Nixon Doctrine, enunciated by the President shortly after his 1968 election, proposed in effect that allies of the United States rely upon regional forces for self-defense, with aid and assistance, but not manpower, from the United States. The one place where the President pledged the continued involvement of American manpower was in the NATO area.

President Nixon's emphasis on regionalism coincided with a widely held impression that international bipolarity was becoming modified. In the strategic nuclear sense, this was not so, for the United States and the Soviet Union remained preeminently the world's nuclear powers, and would remain so at least until the 1980s. However, apart from the strategic nuclear question, Chinese testing of nuclear weapons dramatized the entry of that nation into the great power category. In addition, the great Japanese economic miracle—not a new event but one which had been going on for well over a decade—had finally entered world consciousness and Japanese consciousness as well, now that Japan had the second largest gross national product in the non-Communist world.

Further, by 1972, England's Conservative government had moved her into the Common Market. If the addition of England to the Common Market meant that it would be closer to the union of nations emphasized by de Gaulle than to the supranational entity desired by Monnet, still perhaps Europe was an entity to be reckoned with in an industrial and monetary, if not yet a military, sense.

It appeared that a new pentagonal arrangement would be imposed on the basic military bipolarity—one involving the U.S.S.R., the U.S., Europe, Japan, and China. The Nixon Doctrine implies this view of

31

the emerging macroframework of world politics. Basing foreign policy upon such a view is a reasonable enterprise, for the macroframework of world politics is predictable in principle. Genuine surprises will surely occur in detail, and may even occur with respect to the macroframework itself, although in this respect many such failures of anticipation represent failures in analysis.

For example, in the mid-1950s, the image of the Soviet bloc as monolithic was prevalent, and few foresaw the strains in NATO. Yet other views were even then available. In a work of which this writer was coauthor, *United States Foreign Policy: 1945-1955,* it was noted that

> the pattern of objectives and policies that the United States developed in the first five years after the Second World War was clearly based on a judgment about the nature of the international system in which it was operating. The system was seen as rapidly tending toward a bipolar structure. . . . it is equally important to state that this pattern of purposes and action could not be continued into the indefinite future unless the international system continued to conform to the original estimate. This study has been explicit in concluding that this condition has not been met. It concludes, in short, that, at some point in the mid-1950s, a reverse trend, an evolution away from bipolarity, began. Such a reversal was natural enough, for in a system that is still made up of national states, concentrations of power, unless they are quickly turned into action, create resistances. . . . Both the Soviet Union and the United States—the latter in spite of the support initially given its purposes—became the objects of these accumulating resistances.[1]

In *System and Process in International Politics,* published one year later (1957), this writer noted that "when a member actor is as strong as China, the directive element of the system does not function too well. In fact, were all the member actors related like China and the Soviet Union, the bloc would have to be regarded as nonhierarchical since then the geographic distinctions would far outweigh the functional crosscutting taking place within the bloc." [2]

The ink was hardly dry on *United States Foreign Policy: 1945-1955* when the Hungarian revolution broke out. A mere three years after the publication of *System and Process in International Politics* the rupture between China and the Soviet Union became public knowledge.

---

[1] Reitzel, Kaplan, and Coblenz, *U.S. Foreign Policy,* pp. 462-63.
[2] Kaplan, *System and Process in International Politics,* p. 79.

It was in that same period that the difficulties within NATO became accentuated and that the rupture with Gaullist France began to incubate.

The Macroframework, the Soviet Question, and NATO

If, in 1945 and 1955, one had to consider the Soviet problem to understand the problems of West Europe, the situation is little different in 1972. NATO—as contrasted with Europe—would not exist in the absence of Soviet-controlled Eastern Europe. The alternatives for NATO and for Europe, therefore, cannot be considered in isolation from the alternatives for the Soviet Union.

Through the early 1950s, the Soviet Union and the United States sought to build systems of security directed at reducing the uncertainties resulting from the Second World War. The mid- and late-1950s saw the two great powers striving desperately to patch up the flaws in these systems. As is usual in such circumstances the actors were uncertain about the proper directions to follow: toward some measure of decentralization in bloc structure or toward control of internal bloc problems by an attempt to bring external problems under tighter control.

The Berlin crises of the late 1950s may have been overdetermined. They may have represented attempts to test the will of the West. They may have been defensive counteractions against the course of events in Western Europe. Or they may have represented frantic Soviet efforts to reduce bloc dissidence by creating external crises. In any event, these motivations would have been given relatively little credence by Western statesmen in the 1950s, for the then current conceptions accepted the conspiratorial view that the Soviet Union was preparing for aggressive war. Buffeted by bloc dissidence, the specific rift with China, and the strategic superiority of the United States, the Soviet Union, however, likely viewed itself as beleaguered.

The decline of American power in the late 1960s has moderated these Soviet fears as have successful Soviet moves in the Mediterranean, the *Ostpolitik* of Brandt, and the growth of Soviet military power. On the other hand, the Soviet experience with China has served to radically change the Soviet view of world communism. The Soviet Union by now has a jaundiced view of genuinely independent Communist states— particularly of those possessing nuclear weapons. In addition, it may not be entirely unhappy with a Western Europe that is governed by "decadent" bourgeois governments that are responsive to public opinion

33

and consumer demands. At any event, it is clearly unwilling under current conditions to run any serious risks to impose its control over Western Europe.

As bipolarity has diminished, both the United States and the Soviet Union have come up against striking limits on their ability to produce change elsewhere in the world. Their major problem is to adjust to this reduction of influence in ways that are not threatening to their security or to their national values. Unless the United States handles its international affairs incompetently or adopts a defense budget that gravely impairs its conventional and/or strategic nuclear capabilities, this should produce a more decentralized world order with strong regional overtones.

The current period may see the Soviet Union and the United States with apparently cooperative interests in controlling and regulating change in such ways that their interests are not directly and massively challenged. This joint interest might be viewed as an effort to establish a condominium and, in this form, undoubtedly it would be justly resented by many other nations. If, on the other hand, these groping efforts to accommodate Soviet-American world interests are seen as the alternative to an active condominium in which direct control of the international system, rather than merely of the process of change, is at issue, they might be understood as an effort to construct a more decentralized world order. Yet joint U.S.-U.S.S.R. declarations that pointedly ignore the principle of self-determination in Europe do not reassure our NATO allies.

The major area in which Soviet-American accommodation is required is Europe, for in the current stage of history, this is the area of the world with the greatest concentration of skilled manpower and economic productivity outside the Soviet Union and the United States. This is what makes the NATO problem central to any consideration of Soviet-American relations. This is one of two important areas, the other being China, where the Soviet Union may be tempted to solve its problems, if they reach crisis proportions, by aggressive means—if the American position has been impaired either by political incompetence or by unwise military decisions.

We do not, however, suggest an actual Soviet invasion of Western Europe as the most likely response to crisis and opportunity, although that cannot entirely be precluded. If the cohesion of NATO further weakens, if the military superiority of the Warsaw Treaty Organization forces over NATO is further enhanced, and if the global nuclear strategic balance swings even further in favor of the Soviet Union, then a number of conditions might occur in which the Soviet Union would be encouraged to employ political blackmail and threats against Western Europe to achieve its political objectives, much as Khrushchev unsuccessfully attempted to do in the middle and late 1950s. In this respect, if economic rivalry and political suspicion increase between the United States and the European members of NATO, if leftist coalitions gain ground in France and Italy, if the left wing of the German Social Democratic party increases in strength, and if the American will to act seems visibly to weaken, such possibilities become more than remote. They might be triggered by a Yugoslav succession crisis, by an attempt to bring Rumania into line, by a crisis within the German Democratic Republic, or by some variant of the Czechoslovak spring in some other Eastern European country—Poland, for instance. Subsidiary decisions that might increase the likelihood of such a crisis could include reductions in the American carrier fleet, successive reductions in the American force structure in Europe, and neglect of the strategic nuclear balance. The proposed McGovern defense budget serves as an example of the type of incompetent military planning decisions that might facilitate such a crisis. The growing economic discord between the United States and Europe provides multiple opportunities for political incompetence, any of which could threaten much of the remaining cohesion of NATO.

Western European Problems

Since the early 1960s the growing political divergencies within Western Europe and between the nations of Western Europe and the United States have become emphasized. In part, this is a product of political stability, economic prosperity, and détente. Should the Soviet support for détente be reversed, attitudes toward NATO might change concordantly and in ways which would reinvigorate it. On the other hand, independent political processes are in process that may prove irreversible, even in such an eventuality.

In many respects, we are returning to the uncertainties of the middle and late 1940s, although with an interesting twist, for these uncertainties are occurring within the framework of world pressures that make for détente and cooperation rather than for conflict, at least in their immediate impact. Yet these uncertainties do create serious doubts about the future that, under some circumstances, might tempt forcible or threatening responses from one of the superpowers.

In Western Europe, the nation most visibly on the front lines of East-West tensions is the Federal Republic of Germany. Chancellor Willy Brandt has recently been reelected and appears firmly in power for a number of years. In any event, his policy of *Ostpolitik* was accepted by his Christian Democratic opposition with only minor qualifications. *Ostpolitik* represents an obvious response to the partial failures of postwar-Germany policy. The integrated Europe that Adenauer hoped for as a substitute for a reunited Germany suffered at least a temporary death with the ascension to power of General de Gaulle. The European defense community was stillborn. On the other hand, the growing strength of NATO never produced German unity. The Hallstein doctrine that sought to isolate the German Democratic Republic eventually lost its usefulness.

Moreover, as the flush of vigorous anticommunism passed its peak and receded in the West, it could hardly be expected to motivate West German policy indefinitely. If Nixon went to Moscow and Peking, how far behind could Brandt remain? Yet these very measures, by emphasizing détente, deemphasized NATO. If, in addition, American ground commitments to Germany are reduced, the provocative entailment of the American presence may become more visible to Germans than its defensive potential. These already may be among the pressures stimulating the youth left within the Social Democratic party. Apparently they are not entirely without some counterparts on the right wing in German politics, although the solutions sought by the extremes would be different in content.

Like the other actors on the scene, West Germany is walking a narrow path. Too sharp a move in one direction may weaken NATO irreparably. Too sharp a step in the other direction may threaten détente and *Ostpolitik*. Although presently supported by broad majorities in both major parties, the equilibrium may be fragile, if not exactly unstable.

Although France is now cooperating more with NATO than under de Gaulle, the absence of joint command structures impairs the authority of NATO action in Western Europe. French policy proceeds in resolutely logical fashion from irrational premises. The French recognize their need for a United States presence in Europe to offset both the Germans and the Russians. Although favoring a general European security conference, they are vigorously opposing mutual balanced force reduction (MBFR) discussions because they do not wish to countenance a reduction in American forces in Europe. Yet an agreement with the Soviet Union on modest reductions may be required if the United States is to put a floor under senatorial pressure for major reductions. The French continue to pursue an independent nuclear policy for which they lack an adequate resource base. They point out that in the last resort American weapons might not be used in defense of France. That the argument applies equally well to the West Germans escapes French attention and, in any event, is not a realistic consideration from their standpoint, for the West Germans are not clamoring for nuclear weapons. Yet this contradiction in French policy remains a potential festering sore.

Recent public opinion polls in France show the possibility of a parliamentary victory by a left-wing coalition. As this coalition would include the French Communist party, it would not likely add to the solidarity of NATO. Even though this coalition failed at its last trial, the coherence of French and NATO policy appears open to question.

There is the danger of a leftist coalition succeeding in Italy, with its evident threat to NATO, a threat the Italian Communist party has made explicit. The intention of the Scandinavian countries to opt out of any NATO strategy that raises nuclear implications also produces difficulties. Although in some ways the Scandinavian members of NATO are its most loyal adherents, desiring the United States as an offset to the major European powers, their attitudes toward nuclear weapons constitute a potential weakness, particularly during crises.

Soviet moves into the Mediterranean, potential conflicts between Greece and Turkey, internal American dissent over our home-basing of the fleet in Greece, and senatorial reactions to Spain and Portugal create numerous problems for political and strategic coherence in Western policy in the European area. The less adequate the NATO military posture, the more important these political deficiencies will appear. The stronger our security measures and the greater the will of the United States to enforce them, the less prominent the pulls and strains of conflicting national policies will appear. A less resolute American position and a weaker defense posture will make NATO appear less valuable for defense, more provocative to the Soviet Union, and a greater impediment to détente.

At the moment no alternatives to the present NATO posture are seen as obvious improvements, and the members of NATO are loathe to call too much attention to the deficiencies in the organization. Yet lurking in the awareness of each is some recognition of the inadequacy of the present position and some readiness to consider alternatives.

Warsaw Treaty Organization

Several of the Soviet Union's WTO "partners" seem quite responsive to measures for changing the present political circumstances in Europe. Rumania is actively supporting a European security conference and proposing limitations on bloc manuevers without notice and on the use of force. These limitations would be quite consistent with the dissuasion strategy proposed in the volume. The Rumanians have also been pushing for the equality of all powers in the conference and appear to be using the conference not to stabilize the status quo in Europe but to mobilize support for change in ways that ultimately would lead to the breakup of the two bloc structures. At times the Yugoslavs seem friendly toward these Rumanian efforts, although recent Yugoslav actions appear more concerned with the possibility of ideological slackness within Yugoslavia than with maintenance of Yugoslav neutrality between the blocs.

Thus, the Soviet Union has very interesting problems with its bloc partners. Of all the eastern European states, only Bulgaria has genuinely warm relations with the Soviet Union, and even she appears partly receptive to a new state of affairs in Europe. A brutal intervention was required to repress Czechoslovak aspirations in 1968. Rumania, although paying lip service to the bloc in terms of international policy, pursues internal autonomy and irritatingly seeks ties with the Chinese. Poland under Gierek is increasingly restive.

The East Germans are disliked by the Russians. Although the Russians are attempting to stabilize the East German regime, for a unified non-Communist Germany would seem threatening to the Soviet Union, the Russians likely recognize the dangers of their present linkage to the East German regime. East Germany is least dangerous when permanently divided from West Germany; this is undoubtedly one of the reasons why the Russians are more interested than the West in a formal recognition of two German states. However, the East Germans remain *Germans*. From the Russian point of view, they represent a form of economic efficiency and political determination that poses a potential threat to Russian security. The East German regime must continue to tread a thin line to remain safe for, and from, the Russians. There must be sufficient political consensus behind the regime to make unlikely a new uprising such as that of 1953. On the other hand, there must not be sufficient consensus behind the regime to permit the East Germans to move toward the type of independence the Rumanians have manifested. Although the presence of Soviet divisions in East Germany now precludes moves toward independence by the East Germans equivalent to those of the Rumanians, the danger of such a development is always present. Unlike the West Germans, with their democratic regime, the East Germans could use the principles of democratic centralism to mobilize their economy and war machine in a way that the suspicious Russians might easily equate with the Chinese threat. To permit the collapse of the East German regime and its absorption into West Germany would threaten the entire eastern European position of the Soviet Union, the internal legitimacy of its regime, and its defense structure in the west. Yet the East German regime is a potential threat to the Soviet Union. The Soviet Union possesses no genuine solution for this dilemma, and that is an additional reason why at some point a westward expansion of Soviet influence in Europe might become extremely tempting to the Soviet leadership.

Thus, just as NATO is confronted with a cross-conflict of national policies, the WTO is beset with similar problems. The Russians no doubt could bring this under control by military means, but at an enormous price in terms of national consensus within the involved states, détente with the West, and security in the confrontation with China. Moreover, this could be done only at a high price in terms of the legitimacy of the internal Soviet regime, for although the action would not likely create an active opposition within the Soviet Union, it would do grave damage to the ideological basis of its polity and its faith in its future. The cost in terms of internal Russian development and economic progress would be difficult to bear for the Russian people. Changes in popular attitudes, even if they did not produce political dissidence, would threaten the economic strength, and thereby the military security, of the Soviet Union. Thus, the Soviet Union has no easy solution to this problem.

The Internal Soviet Process

The Soviet Union is faced with a myriad of problems with respect to its security on its European front (and on its Asian front as well). It has major nationality and minority problems in European Russia, with Ukrainians, Jews, and the Baltic peoples constituting large bodies of potential dissidents.

In addition to these problems, the Soviet Union is developing a weak but definite consumer economy. By American or European standards, the Russian economy is mobilized for war with little consideration of consumer preferences. By past Soviet standards, however, the improvements in the situation of the consumer have set loose personal desires and expectations that could be controlled only at immense political cost, and even then only if there is a major overt external threat. Consumer production is fast becoming an extremely important, and perhaps vital, buttress to regime legitimacy—a legitimacy that is in serious question.

Apart from the legitimacy that successful governance confers, a Communist one-party system has two main theoretical sources of legitimacy. The first source lies in the nature of the class antagonisms that are postulated by fundamental Marxian theory. It is widely known within the Soviet Union that this Marxian view, so intimately related to the concept of surplus value, is increasingly being discredited by the modern economic techniques of accounting and management being employed within the Soviet Union. The second source of legitimacy rests on the conception that the party possesses a monopoly of scientific political truth. This prop has been weakened beyond repair by the challenge of China.

There is no great body of support for establishing a free enterprise system in Russia or for adopting the formal processes of political democracy of a Western European variety. However, the Soviet regime is confronted with the possibility of serious challenges if it loses economic momentum, and it has only limited support for external adventures. On the other hand, the regime cannot afford to appear to have lost control of events, for continued success is its only ground for being. Therefore, unless the regime is willing to relinquish power, it requires continued success. Success can come through adapting to change or through preventing it. Each of these courses entails risks and costs.

There is no evidence, and no reason to believe, that the Soviet leadership either can, or wishes to, give up the levers of internal or external power. There is considerable evidence to support the hypothesis that the Soviet Union long hesitated before making its decision to engage in a military operation in Czechoslovakia in 1968. The political price was high. Yet, if it had not intervened, the military would have sharply noted the consequences for the Soviet defensive posture in Europe. Moreover, Soviet nonintervention would have been perceived as a failure of will rather than as a principled decision. Dissident forces would have been encouraged both in the Soviet Union and in the bloc. The next similar case—and it would have been encouraged quickly by the success of the first—would have emboldened external sources of assistance and would have threatened a crisis for the Soviet regime. Greater fear would have produced a much more brutal crackdown and the danger of war. No major element in the Politburo likely would support a liberal solution in this severe type of crisis. Current divergencies of opinion in the Politburo primarily are over how to avoid these severe threats to the regime and its interests. Although there are some value differences, primarily the argument is over differing estimates of the risks, costs, and gains potentially involved in alternative policies.

There is little reliable information about the factionalism in the Soviet Politburo. There is likely a conservative faction within the Kremlin that sees a solution to its problems in a policy that erodes NATO without impairing effective Soviet control in Eastern Europe. This erosion would do three things for the Soviet Union: it would permit it to turn its attention to the Chinese challenge; it would remove hope from the Eastern European satellites that freedom from Soviet control was genuinely possible; and it would reduce internal legitimacy problems by manifesting great competence in the pursuit of Soviet power. Likely there is also a powerful centrist faction in the Soviet Politburo that sees excessive risks in this extreme policy. This centrist faction probably agrees that initial successes could be achieved by such a policy, but it sees in it the dangers of a vast American reaction, of an intensive arms race, and of an eventual reinvigoration of NATO. This faction probably desires minimal change in Europe and an increased Soviet potential for coping with the Chinese challenge and with internal economic problems. This faction probably believes that such a policy would produce sufficient relaxation to moderate both internal nationality problems and bloc cohesion problems. Some in this faction might be sympathetic to slow changes in the cohesion of the Warsaw Pact, coordinately with the removal of the United States from Western Europe, in the hope that this would improve the political and economic relations of the Soviet

41

Union with its Eastern European partners. There may also be a third faction in the Soviet Politburo—probably the smallest of the three— that hopes to see an evolution of the Soviet regime itself. This faction may not be democratic in a Western European sense, but it probably aspires toward a situation in which Lenin's description of administration as accountancy comes closer to expressing political reality in the Soviet Union than does the current situation. This faction is humanistic in its philosophy and likely desires to see a serious reduction in the coercive power of the Soviet state.

Soviet Attitudes Toward NATO

All three of these factions would manifest some similarities in their basic posture toward NATO and a European security agreement. The first faction would see European security as a means of eroding American interest in NATO, as undermining European support for a continued American presence, and as a propaganda tool for producing changes in Western Europe that are favorable to the extension of Soviet power. The centrist faction would see European security as a technique for serious negotiations with the West. It likely would have maximal and minimal objectives, and likely would be pragmatic in its negotiation of these. It would be willing to run only minor risks concerning Soviet control of the Warsaw Treaty Organization states; even these would be taken only in response to concessions by NATO. This centrist faction would pay close attention to national security arguments by the Soviet generals. It would watch carefully for risks and strains within the East European states. It would watch carefully the possible development of economic ties between eastern and western Europe that might be threatening to relations between the Soviet Union and the WTO states. It would bargain hard and from positions of strength. The third faction would see European security negotiations primarily from the standpoint of arms control and internal liberalization. It would be wary of possible Western tricks, for its members are dedicated Communists and are concerned to maintain socialism in the Soviet Union. On the other hand, they might be prepared to go too far too fast. They are inclined to believe that once the process of liberalization truly begins, it will be difficult to stop. They perhaps underestimate the extent to which the process might get out of hand both within the Soviet Union and in Europe and, thus, lead to Thermidorean responses.

These possible Soviet positions are expressed schematically. A number of qualifications need to be made in order to assess the practicability of Western responses. In the first place, as in other political systems, many of the Soviet leaders who take these positions do so because it is presently advantageous for them, given their past histories and commitments, in terms of intraparty politicking. Many of them, particularly in the first two factions, would find it quite easy to change their positions if this were politically advantageous. Secondly, even to the extent that the positions are seriously held by the participants, belief in them depends upon the concatenation of conditions under which they are to be implemented. For instance, significant evidence concerning a lack of will or incompetence in leadership circles in the United States might turn a centrist into a hardliner. He might believe the risks to be lower and the potential gains higher. Or he might fear American incompetence and the concomitant risk that the entire process of international relations would get out of control or produce anarchy, a condition that is both attractive and frightening to the Russian mind.

Each of the three positions depends upon a series of (mostly implicit) assumptions concerning the political process in every major nation and the alternatives genuinely available to the Soviet Union. Each, therefore, is subject to modification as evidence begins to conflict with one or more of these hypotheses. The human mind being what it is, the major contours of positions do not shift until there is a substantial accumulation of evidence, but the beliefs underlying these positions are not purely abstract. Obviously, the positions are not held in the same way by each member of a "faction" in the Soviet Union. Thus, for evidential, and also for political, reasons the factions are subject to marginal shift.

To make this process more explicit, let us construct an example. Suppose that the centrist faction was intending to set in motion a process that would lead to the elimination of both military blocs in Europe. One might believe, if one knew this, that proposing such a solution would facilitate agreement with these leaders. And perhaps agreement would be reached. On the other hand, however, such an offer by the West might convince some of the centrist leaders that they could safely adopt the posture of those hardliners who wish to use this process to solve the Soviet Union's security problem in a simpler, more predictable, and less ambiguous fashion through the Finlandization of Western Europe. This could occur even if the proposal were viewed only as an evidence of a disposition of mind on the part of Western political leaders. As we know, proposals set in motion political consequences, many of which escape subsequent control. Proposals by NATO for accommodation with the Soviet Union could make far more difficult the adoption of measures designed to improve the military situation in NATO, particularly if these security negotiations were to take place over a long period of time, although never quite coming to satisfactory conclusions. Thus they might create an opportunity too tempting to resist. Moreover, to make their compromises acceptable to the hard-liners, the centrist faction may have to demonstrate that an effort was made to achieve more.

Suppose the Soviet leaders genuinely desire a general European security conference precisely to avoid a bloc confrontation. Yet, since they cannot know how the conference will come out, they may find it advantageous for a number of reasons to exploit the natural divisions in the less hegemonial NATO bloc and also to exploit the political divisions that occur within multiparty systems. In the first case, the prospect of the desired agreement has opened up an even more agree-able alternative for the Soviet Union. In the second case, the eventual agreement is problematical and the advantages of using the conference for other purposes become difficult to resist. In both cases, Soviet motives change (for the worse from a Western point of view).

This does not mean that negotiations are to be avoided, but only that they need to be analyzed from a viewpoint that takes these inter-actions into account. A failure to approach such negotiations in a sophisticated fashion is likely to lead to their failure or to other unfortu-nate consequences. The Soviet leaders themselves distrust negotiations with naive opposite numbers precisely because of their unpredictable results. Uncertainty is always a threat to statesmen as conservative as the Russians.

4

The Current Situation

Despite the large Soviet military buildup in central Europe, it is extremely doubtful that the Soviet Union has any intention of attacking in the west. It is too preoccupied with China, with problems of internal economic development, and with problems of bloc management to wish the further embarrassment of a successful war that installed Communist regimes in Western Europe. However, despite these qualifications, the United States and the current bourgeois regimes in Western Europe, and particularly that of West Germany, do have important conflicts of interest with the Soviet Union and with some members of its bloc. This is recognized by Soviet leaders.[1]

One cannot exclude the possibility that some unexpected event or crisis in bloc management may create a strong incentive for Soviet pressure on the West—an incentive that would be increased by a predominance of power in the Warsaw Pact. Under these circumstances, the Soviet Union might be encouraged to make demands that, if unmet, might seriously increase the risk of war.

The Geopolitical Situation of Europe

Because of the European orientation of our history courses, we tend to think of Europe as a genuine continent, whereas it is merely a peninsula on the Eurasian land mass. Our images of armies marching back and forth across the face of Europe leads us to forget that the distance from

---

[1] See the important article by G. A. Arbatov, director of the U.S.A. Institute, reprinted in *Orbis*, vol. 15, no. 1 (Spring 1971), pp. 134-53.

the East German border to Paris is roughly the width of the state of Pennsylvania. Using the antiquated equipment of World War II, the Germans quickly moved to the Atlantic during the Ardennes offensive. In the age of the jet plane, the fast tank, and mobile armored divisions, Europe is a toy war ground. It lacks space for depth of maneuver. Moreover, in the nuclear age, even relatively small numbers of thermonuclear weapons would be capable of turning the nations of Western Europe into dust—a fact that Khrushchev often pointed out. In both world wars, the great American economic machine had time to crank up and restore the situation. Even so, the United States hardly would have been capable of carrying out the amphibious invasion of Western Europe if Germany had not also been occupied with the Russians in the east. Moreover, that invasion was not met by modern aviation. These are matters that rarely occur to Americans, but they can never lie far beneath the consciousness of Europeans. Independence requires confidence.

An increasing predominance on the part of the Warsaw Pact, or a diminishing American presence in Europe, might incline the Soviet Union to expect Western Europe to concede a Soviet primacy that would preclude independent foreign policies that conflicted with important Soviet objectives either in Europe or elsewhere in the world. This postulated condition is essentially the current situation of Finland, although the particular relationship between Finland and the Soviet Union, which resulted from the compromises agreed to after the Second World War, rests on a treaty arrangement. Finland is an independent country but the Finnish political parties recognize the need to adjust to the Soviet presence. Often the Soviet Union does not need to state its requirements, for the various Finnish political groupings anticipate them.

The Czechoslovak coup of 1948 serves as a grim reminder that the Soviet Union has employed military threats and local Communists to demoralize a nation and to produce a regime change. This case has obvious parallels to the technique that Sir Lewis Namier called chemical dissolution and which was used by Adolf Hitler. Finlandization is a more moderate method of obtaining one's way but it works even better when there is an example of a harsher method that has already been used.

External control of policy is a matter of degree. Most nations would find it difficult to refrain from implementing their policies, including those related to increased security, when the means for influencing other nations are readily available. The nations of western Europe have a multiplicity of parties with conflicting interests and conflicting views of the domestic situation and of the external world. In the absence of overt and obvious external threats, their governments have an understandable interest in pursuing domestic measures conducive to popularity. Even apart from the existence of Communist parties, there likely would be some groupings within each nation sympathetic to specific Russian policies. It would take great abnegation for the Soviet Union not to use these advantages in securing support for its policies. The United States makes use of similar opportunities in the WTO to the limited extent that they are available. However, authoritarian nations have more effective levers for policy control, and pluralistic democracies present greater target opportunities. Central government control over trade, commerce, the exchange of persons, and many other areas of life provides Communist countries with means of influence largely, but not totally, unavailable to the West.

The current degree of Finnish independence is supported by the existence of a strong NATO. A relative, but sharply reduced, independence of Western Europe in the circumstance of great Soviet predominance might be supported by an active and vigorous American war potential in the western hemisphere. The situation, therefore, perhaps would not be entirely irretrievable if Western Europe were Finlandized, but only a fool would fail to recognize that a major unfavorable change in the macrostructure of world politics would have occurred.

It is perhaps true that a great Soviet military predominance in Europe might not produce Finlandization or that the existence of a credible defensive posture in Western Europe might not avoid it if great alliance or internal political difficulties arose. Yet, if a credible defensive posture is neither a necessary nor a sufficient condition for the avoidance of Finlandization, it is surely a condition that minimizes its likelihood. Therefore, even in that case in which our conception of the strategic/political process of international politics is much broader than that achieved through military analysis, a preliminary survey of the more obvious comparisons in military potential is unquestionably essential to an understanding of the prospects for independence and influence of the European members of NATO.

47

The Military Balance

The best unofficial estimates of the forces in NATO and in the Warsaw Pact are given in *The Military Balance,* a publication of the International Institute of Strategic Studies (IISS). These are based upon information coming from a wide variety of sources and, although not completely accurate, are probably as good as the public record will allow. The most recent issue of *The Military Balance,* published at the end of 1972, probably underestimates the current Warsaw Pact advantage, but it is sufficiently good for the purposes of our discussion. (See Table 1.) If the French-based forces in Germany under separate agreement with NATO are added to the NATO figure for northern and central Europe, approximately 40,000 additional troops, some of which may be stationed in France, would be available.

Table 1

COMPARISON OF NATO AND WARSAW PACT FORCES

Category	Northern and Central European Forces			Southern European Forces		
	NATO	Warsaw Pact	(Of which are Soviet)	NATO	Warsaw Pact	(Of which are Soviet)
Ground formations (in division equivalents)						
Armored	9	31	(21)	6	8	(3)
Infantry (mechanized and airborne)	15	36	(20)	31	19	(4)
Combat and direct support troops	580	1,000	(650)	530	350	(90)
Main battle tanks	6,000	16,000	(10,000)	2,100	5,200	(1,600)
Operational tactical aircraft						
Light bomber	64	250	(200)	—	30	(30)
Fighter/ground attack	1,200	1,400	(1,100)	450	120	(50)
Interceptor	400	2,100	(1,100)	250	950	(450)
Reconnaissance	400	450	(300)	150	90	(40)
Total	2,064	4,200	(2,700)	850	1,190	(570)

Source: *The Military Balance: 1972-1973* (London: The International Institute for Strategic Studies, 1972), pp. 87-90.

Roughly comparable figures are provided by Drew Middleton's *New York Times* dispatches of 1 and 2 June 1972. In Middleton's figures, NATO forces, including France, are placed at 500,000 troops and 1,800 tactical aircraft, and the Warsaw Pact forces on the central front are estimated at 750,000 men and 3,500 tactical aircraft. According to Middleton, Soviet nuclear forces in central Europe have been equipped with special vehicles and decontamination equipment unmatched in any Western army. Their training for all types of warfare, including nuclear, is extensive. He reports that Soviet forces have been modernized over the past 18 months and that they have received new types of tanks and a new vehicle combining the functions of an armored personnel carrier and a scout car. Their tanks, scout cars, and armored personnel carriers have improved antiaircraft capabilities. Antitank armaments and surface-to-surface missile capabilities have been greatly increased. Artillery, he points out, has been modernized.

The IISS figures show that the Soviet Union has a rather large manpower edge on the central front which includes the important German front. NATO does have an edge in southern Europe, but many of these troops are in Italy, Greece, and Turkey and are not available to the central front. The Russian advantage is understated because of the dispositions of its forces. As the Soviet divisions are organized for shock tactics, far more men are available for direct military activities than these figures indicate. The NATO forces, with better logistic components, are better disposed to fight a long war, provided that their logistic supply lines are not destroyed and provided that they have not been broken up and outflanked by shock maneuvers.

According to the IISS, the Warsaw Pact has a distinct mobilization advantage during the first 30 days of crisis or conflict.[2] Many observers believe that this advantage would be reversed sometime after the sixtieth day of crisis. The Soviet Union has about a three-to-one advantage in tanks. According to the IISS, NATO has an advantage in antitank weapons.[3] This is dubious, but, even if true, it is far outweighed by the fact that the Warsaw Pact tank forces outnumber by many times the NATO antitank weapons.

The Warsaw Pact also has a great advantage in numbers of tactical aircraft. Although NATO aircraft are more sophisticated with longer

[2] *The Military Balance: 1972-1973* (London: The International Institute for Strategic Studies, 1972), pp. 88-89.
[3] Ibid., p. 89.

ranges and heavier payloads, the Soviet-made aircraft are designed to give close support to ground operations,[4] the kind of support the WTO forces would require during attack missions. In addition to interior lines of communication, the Soviet Union has far greater dispersal of, and far more, airfields than NATO.[5]

Although the McNamara Defense Department kept talking of the need of the aggressor to mobilize a three-to-one advantage for a breakthrough on the ground, it perhaps overestimated the capacity of NATO to predict the point of attack and to shift defensive forces to meet it. The defense must spread itself along the front while the attacker can choose the moment and point of attack. The swift movement of Warsaw Pact forces into Czechoslovakia in 1968, and the tactical surprise that was achieved, cast some doubt on the Enthoven-McNamara thesis. The noted French analyst, General Beaufre, believes that under current plans and dispositions a Warsaw Pact attack would reach the Rhine in several days.[6] More optimistic analysts conclude that NATO forces could hold out for four to eight weeks. Even if all the analysts are overly pessimistic, the extent to which these views are held, and the apparent evidence on which they are based, do not support that degree of alliance cohesion and assurance that is politically required. As a consequence, many continental analysts view the American forces as symbolic hostages for the strategic deterrent. General Beaufre suggests instead the employment of small tactical nuclear weapons before the opposing forces are in contact, but regards this as a deterrent rather than as a war-fighting measure.[7] The trouble with deterrent systems that cannot be used during actual combat is that, as the fever pitch of a crisis increases, their threat becomes exposed as a bluff to those who employ them and tends to undermine the will of the defender rather than that of the attacker. A doctrine that may dissuade a potential aggressor from initiating a crisis may in turn persuade the potential defender to make concessions if events, not completely under control, bring it into existence.

---

[4] Ibid.

[5] Ibid., p. 90.

[6] General André Beaufre, "Problems of Strategy and European Security," in *Problems and Strategy and European Security,* paper prepared for the Franco-American Symposium, September 1971. General Beaufre suggests such a battle might be lost in a single day.

[7] Ibid.

The Source of Weakness. The comparative military weakness of NATO forces is not a consequence of lack of manpower or economic resources. With adequate political will, NATO could produce more trained troops than the WTO and it could equip them better. However, there is little political support in either Western Europe or the United States for increasing the levels of military manpower or for purchasing higher levels of military equipment. The absence of an overt Soviet threat and the successful Nixon-Brezhnev summits make it unlikely that NATO forces, which have been suffering depletions of strength in the last few years, will see a reversal of this trend.

In the past several years, there has been a strong effort—which so far has been successfully resisted by President Nixon—in the U.S. Senate, under the leadership of Senator Mansfield, to reduce the American contribution of manpower to NATO. Although this move is argued for on primarily economic grounds, it is difficult to understand how it will reduce the size of the defense budget or improve the balance of payments except in a marginal way. The Mansfield proposal is superficially attractive because, in the absence of a credible war-fighting mission for the NATO forces in Europe, the presence of American troops is largely symbolic. They are there as hostages to insure the American nuclear deterrent. In this sense, although a reduction in their number may communicate a decline in American willingness to support Europe in any form, including use of the deterrent, the argument for retention of the present number of troops is weakened by an inability to demonstrate that it is essential to NATO's war-fighting capability. It is difficult to make the argument that removing troops is a step in the wrong direction when there seems no prospect that one will move in the right direction, and when there appears to be no convincing threat from the Warsaw Pact.

A Suggested Improvement. One important suggestion for improving this situation has been made by Steven L. Canby of the RAND Corporation. Mr. Canby suggests that the incremental costs of maintaining the present American long-war-fighting capability are about half of its total costs. If the United States were to buy the same 60-day capability that the Soviet Union has bought, in effect recognizing that a war cannot be won in the long run if it is lost in the short run, the ability of the NATO forces to blunt a Soviet attack would be greatly increased. There is much to be said for Canby's position. Certainly it would be unwise to

51

strengthen the weak northern flank, as suggested by some analysts, by withdrawals from the central front, which is obviously far more important to the West. On the other hand, it is doubtful that the central front can be held if the northern flank collapses.[8]

Canby's suggestions, if adopted, would help to correct some weaknesses of the current NATO posture. However, even if the reforms Canby suggests are adopted, the NATO forces would not achieve parity with the Soviet Union in war-fighting capability. With the present forces in being, and without any further reductions, the reforms Canby suggests would create a near equivalence in men available for combat during the first phases of a war, if mobilization were not at issue. The Soviet Union would still have an enormous advantage in tanks and tactical aircraft and also in the choice of time and place of attack. Moreover, its mobilization advantage in the first 30 days would improve these prospects considerably. Although it is true that the non-Russian Warsaw Pact forces might not be fully reliable, many of the positions they would hold in the Russian lines would not be critical. The East German forces, which might well be in the thick of the fight, likely would prove highly reliable. Thus, although the pessimistic thesis of General Beaufre can perhaps be excluded, thereby increasing deterrence and decreasing the likelihood of Soviet attack, the vulnerability of NATO would still be great.

Asymmetries and Perspectives. Apart from its military superiority, crisis asymmetries also favor the WTO. Some members of the Politburo may worry about Warsaw Pact maneuvers near the border during periods of crisis, but *Pravda* will carry no article suggesting this. The signs of worry in the West will be expressed openly and there will be public pressures on NATO statesmen, who will feel both a political and a moral requirement to take one last chance for peace. The statements made in the free NATO press will be cited by the Soviet Union, whereas NATO can point only to the actual circumstances of Soviet preparations. Moreover, NATO can do this only with care, for some important political figures in the West are likely to view even this as a provocation of the Warsaw Pact.

If our analysis reveals WTO superiority, it does not follow that the Soviet Union fully understands the impact of that superiority upon

---

[8] Among Canby's writings on the subject, see Steven L. Canby, "NATO Muscle: More Shadow than Substance," *Foreign Policy*, Fall 1972, pp. 38-49.

NATO. The Soviet Union is believed to see its offensive superiority in the central European area, its divisional structure, and its quick-attack mobility as essential offsets to the greater long-term military and industrial mobilization capability of the West. However, long-term superiority will be meaningless to NATO if it loses in the short run. Each bloc, therefore, may see the decisions of the other as threatening and as potentially aggressive. The fact of mirror-imaging, if it is a fact, does not mean that serious security problems do not exist. Both situations and motives change, and both Brezhnev and Nixon recognize that some serious conflicts of genuine interest continue to divide Russia and the United States.

Last-Resort Strategies

With some exercise of the imagination, one can think of last-resort strategies that would surely deter the Soviet Union from attacking in the NATO area. For instance, the United States now possesses the capability to produce large numbers of subkiloton nuclear weapons. If defeated in Europe, the U.S. could release these subkiloton weapons to the conquered Western European populations or drop them behind the iron curtain. If the Soviet Union really believed that the United States would do this, thereby making impracticable not merely a successful occupation but continued rule in Eastern Europe or the Soviet Union, this would surely deter the U.S.S.R. The U.S. could then be sure that it would never have to fight another major war in Europe.

Such a strategy would be extremely ill-advised. It is doubtful that the United States would ever desire to put it into effect. If such weapons were distributed in a Soviet-occupied West Europe, Soviet occupation would become impracticable. However, as the U.S. could not control the final distribution of the weapons, their distribution might, indeed likely would, destroy the possibility of civil government in Western Europe. If the distribution of such weapons were restricted to the Soviet bloc, the risk of that immediate consequence in Western Europe would be avoided. However, communism would not have been replaced with something better; the U.S. would have produced an appalling disaster in the Soviet sphere. Moreover, even if the Soviet Union would not by then have learned how to produce similar weapons, it might use larger nuclear weapons against Western Europe or the United States in retaliation. Even if the United States did not fear these consequences, it certainly would not desire moral responsibility for the consequences of this policy.

This extreme last-resort example demonstrates the basic problem of all doctrines based on deterrence only. If one were willing to implement this strategy, it might work in specific circumstances and thus avoid undeniable evils. However, it is essentially a means for escaping from, rather than for solving, problems. A world in which deterrence strategies proliferate would be a disaster. This is why so many people—although, perhaps, not enough—are appalled by the hijackings of planes and the threatened bombings of buildings. Civil relationships among individuals within nations and between nations demand some minimum in the nature of the horrors we will visit upon each other. Unless we are willing to accept the horrifying consequences, we cannot threaten to blow up the globe or to make civil society impossible (or even threaten somewhat more moderate punishment if our demands are unreasonable). We have a responsibility to construct alternatives to deterrence and to adopt policies the success of which do not depend primarily on massive physical destruction or the disruption of civil society and humane community. If we cannot avoid deterrent strategies and threats entirely, they must be employed within the framework of a broader policy that provides the possibility of alternatives, even in extreme situations.

Requirements for a NATO Strategy

If we agree that the present strategic design for NATO is unsatisfactory, there are still a number of constraints a satisfactory design would have to meet, constraints so stringent that most analysts would doubt that we could satisfy them. Under existing political circumstances, a strategic design better than the present one must not require more men, presently unplanned or futuristic weapons systems, or higher expenditures. It should be effective in war, credibly deterring to possible aggressors during peace, stable during crises, supportive of alliance cohesion, understandable both to professional soldiers and professional politicians, consistent with moves toward détente, and not inconsistent with programs for arms reduction. Moreover, this strategic design must not call for actions that are morally outrageous. If we do not wish to return to the tripwire concept—and it does seem outrageous—the shield must be restored to credibility.

5
The Dissuasion Strategy

The IISS figures on NATO and WTO manpower and weapons configurations—and our analysis of them—show WTO superiority. Political reasons preclude NATO military parity in the current period. The weakness of deterrence-only strategies has been discussed in the last chapter. Yet many believe that deterrence has worked historically in Europe, while others assume a surprise attack and therefore search vainly for solutions within that framework. Both assumptions require brief inquiry before turning to the basic assumptions of a strategy designed to dissuade the WTO allies of the Soviet Union from actively supporting it in an aggressive war in Europe in the NATO area. Even though a Soviet attack is unlikely, Soviet superiority in case of attack is a threat to the political assurance of the European members of NATO and, hence, to the security of the United States.

Has Deterrence Worked in Europe?

It is often argued that deterrence has worked both in Europe and elsewhere in the world. If deterrence has worked so well in the past, perhaps it is appropriate to continue to rely on it. There is a sense in which the argument that deterrence has worked is reasonable. The leaders of the United States and of the Soviet Union obviously are reluctant to get involved in situations that might produce a war in which both are involved. There are strong reasons to believe that fear of the appalling consequences of nuclear war plays at least some role in this shared reluctance.

American memoirs recount the extent to which this constraint operated in the Cuban missile crisis.[1] Some of Khrushchev's remarks, which appear less doubtful than other elements in his memoirs, indicate the constraints he felt in this respect.[2] Yet the incidents for which we have evidence all involve peripheral areas of relatively minor importance to at least one of the two nations. There is no substantial evidence that major war in an area as important as Europe has been deterred by the fear of nuclear weapons, for there is no substantial evidence that either of the two major powers has been motivated to take those types of actions that might have led to war in the absence of nuclear weapons.

Much of the feeling of reprieve in Europe is related to the demolished image of Soviet intentions that was held during the height of the cold war. The fears were real enough. The Forrestal diaries include a March 1948 "eyes only" cable from American intelligence stating that the Russians would not attack within the next six months—hardly a reassuring conclusion.[3] However, Titoist sources reveal that Stalin, who unlike the ebullient Khrushchev was extremely conservative in his foreign policies, had no such intentions in that period. When Tito requested assistance from Stalin to move against Trieste, Stalin denounced him for expecting the Soviet Union to run such enormous risks after having fought such a hard war. The primary requirements of the Soviet Union, Stalin said, were for reconstruction. When the Yugoslavs and Bulgarians suggested that the Greek government-in-exile be recognized during the civil war, Stalin harshly criticized them for "a Comsomalist preventive war policy." If he did speak of possibly another "go at it" in another 20 years, when the Soviet Union would be better prepared,[4] this was far from an operational policy. There was a diversionary war hypothesis at the time of the North Korean attack in June 1950, but no significant evidence for this has ever been produced. This does not prove that pure deterrence will not work in Europe but it does suggest that no direct evidence exists to support the hypothesis that it

[1] Robert F. Kennedy, *Thirteen Days: A Memoir of the Cuban Missile Crisis* (New York: W. W. Norton and Co., 1969), p. 23 and pp. 105-06. Arthur M. Schlesinger, Jr., *A Thousand Days: John F. Kennedy in the White House* (Boston: Houghton-Mifflin Co., 1965), pp. 804-08.

[2] Strobe Talbott, ed. and trans., *Khrushchev Remembers* (Boston: Little, Brown and Co., 1970), p. 500.

[3] Forrestal, *The Forrestal Diaries,* p. 387.

[4] Milovan Djilas, *Conversations with Stalin* (New York: Harcourt, Brace and World, 1962), pp. 181-83.

has worked in the past. And Europe is not a peripheral area for either Russia or the United States.

Surprise Attack and Prewar Deterrence

The fear of surprise attack is related in part to NATO's requirement for several months mobilization time to approach parity with the Warsaw Treaty Organization. Yet no war in the last hundred years has begun "out of the blue." The Nazi attack on Poland was preceded by formal demands and a considerable period of crisis, as was the Russian attack on Finland. The Japanese attack on Pearl Harbor occurred after a long crisis. Even the two Israeli attacks on Egypt in 1956 and 1967 were preceded by a considerable period of tension, including, in the latter case, Egyptian actions such as the closure of the Strait of Tiran that might well have been understood as *casus belli*. The Japanese timetable for Pearl Harbor was delayed for more than a month because of disagreements over the prospects for a political settlement with the United States, despite the extremely critical shortages of fuel to which the Japanese were subject. Although one cannot exclude in principle the possibility of an attack without demands or a preceding condition of crisis, past experience suggests that this is a negligible prospect.

The planning of attacks is often subject to delays imposed by disagreements over policies or prospects even during the course of a war. Despite our image of Adolf Hitler as the model of a totalitarian dictator, the Ardennes offensive was delayed for over five months by disagreement with the German general staff. Thus, decision making is not a monolithic process even during war, and there may be pauses during which intrawar deterrence can be applied.

The fact that strategic surprise never occurs does not mean that tactical surprise is never achieved. The United States knew the Japanese were going to attack but did not expect an attack at Pearl Harbor.[5] Stalin refused to believe that Hitler would attack the Soviet Union as early as he did, and to the end, attempted to avoid provocation.[6] The Egyptian air force was caught on the ground even though Egypt knew

---

[5] Joseph C. Grew, *Turbulent Era: A Diplomatic Record of Forty Years, 1904-1945*, vol. 2, ed. Walter Johnson (London: Hammond, Hammond and Co., Ltd., 1953), pp. 1282-1289.

[6] Alexander Werth, *Russia at War, 1941-1945* (New York: G. P. Dutton and Co., 1964), pp. 119-23 and pp. 276-77.

that it had provoked the Israelis to the point of war. The Czechoslovaks were surprised by the invasion by the Warsaw Pact powers despite the maneuvers on their border because they believed that they had achieved a political settlement.

The case of Czechoslovakia in 1968 is very interesting for two important reasons. In the first place, there is reason to believe that the surprise for the Czechoslovaks resulted less from the deliberate employment of a ruse by the Russians than from the inability of the Soviet Union to achieve agreement within its Politburo over this issue. Secondly, NATO postponed its Bavarian maneuvers in order not to provoke the Russians. In this case, NATO was dissuaded from taking actions that would have improved its readiness had the Russians used the occasion to attack in Western Europe.

Thus, the Czechoslovak case emphasizes two very important facts. In the first place, decision making within the Politburo and within the Warsaw Pact prior to a decision to attack may be extremely complex and subject to a variety of influences, some of which may be subject to NATO control. In the second place, NATO can use the period of crisis not only to improve its war-fighting posture, but it also can attempt to use it to avoid conflict. The two objectives may turn out to be in actual, if not in necessary, conflict. This means that a strategic posture consistent with effective war-fighting but not consistent with negotiations for peace during a crisis may be counterproductive. Moreover, it is important to be able to use crisis warning effectively to avoid war *and* to prepare for it, if it occurs.

The Rationale for Dissuasion

If political constraints do not permit NATO to achieve parity in military strength with the Warsaw Treaty Organization, it must find a different solution to its problem. The IISS charts on the vital statistics of the central European confrontation between NATO and the Warsaw Pact show that, even without the improvements in NATO divisional dispositions suggested by Canby, dissuasion of Russia's WTO partners from participating in an attack upon the West, from holding static positions on central front lines, or from interfering with NATO flanking maneuvers would remove the advantage of the Soviet Union in weaponry and manpower. If, in addition, Canby's suggestions were adopted, NATO would possess an extremely effective defensive posture. If the measures used to dissuade the WTO allies of the Soviet Union also delayed the Soviet decision process for more than 60 days, NATO would have an opportunity—if it could find the political means to employ it—to use its long-term mobilization advantage to even improve upon the previously postulated defensive strength. As the factors that produce delay also decrease the likelihood of a successful offensive, the incentive for an attack correspondingly decreases.[7]

Obstacles to Dissuasion

There are several aspects of the current NATO force posture that are inconsistent with dissuasion of the WTO allies of the Soviet Union because they tie together the fates of the U.S.S.R. and its WTO allies during the course of a war. Because these same force postures invite Soviet preemption, they are provocative during a crisis—even if they have some deterrence value in the absence of a crisis—and consequently are destructive of NATO alliance cohesion.

Pershings and QRAs. The two force systems that have these effects are the Pershing missiles and the quick reaction aircraft. The Pershing system of short-range offensive missiles has a range of 460 miles according to the International Institute of Strategic Studies. Although that range would barely reach Russian borders, the Russians are hardly likely to view the range figure as sacrosanct. Therefore, from a Russian point of view, Pershing must be viewed as a weapon that can hit the westernmost parts of the Soviet Union. From the standpoint of Russia's Eastern European partners, Pershing is a weapon directed primarily against their territory. Because of the large size of the Pershing warhead, the estimated 250 Pershings deployed with NATO forces would be capable of enormous collateral damage to Eastern Europe, even if their targets were purely military. Thus, because Pershing does not discriminate between Russian military targets and collateral damage in Eastern

---

[7] Needless to say, there is an extensive debate among experts on the relative mobilization rates of NATO and the Warsaw Treaty Organization. Therefore, the exact period of time during which the superior WTO short-term mobilization superiority would operate and beyond which the long-term NATO mobilization superiority would come into play is also a matter of dispute. However, that a significant delay in WTO attack plans is of great potential assistance to the defensibility of the NATO area is, as far as I know, not questioned by any recognized authorities.

Europe, its inclusion in NATO war-fighting plans tends to tie together the fates of the Soviet Union and its WTO allies.

Given the low state of security in West Germany, it is likely that most of the Pershing firing positions are known to Warsaw Pact planners. Therefore, Pershing increases the incentive of the Soviet Union to strike first with nuclear weapons. This very provocative fact will be noticed quickly by West European publics and statesmen during a period of crisis. If they do not notice it on their own, the Soviet Union will surely call it to their attention. There is a strong probability either that Pershing will be forced out in a crisis as statesmen take one last chance for peace, or that it will cause such dissension in NATO that it will gravely injure alliance cohesion during crisis bargaining. In either case it will have weakened, rather than strengthened, NATO.

A second source of difficulty exists in the quick reaction aircraft, commonly referred to as QRAs. Except for the small fraction of the QRA force on ready alert, these aircraft are extremely vulnerable to a first strike. An attacker would have a strong temptation to hit them first, for they carry nuclear bombs in the megaton range. Although capable of hitting the Soviet Union, thereby increasing the incentive of the Soviet Union to strike first, they would probably do most of their damage in Eastern Europe. Thus, they bind Eastern Europe to the Soviet Union and interfere with NATO's requirement of separating the interests of the WTO allies from those of the Soviet Union. Although the warheads are kept under American control, QRA aircraft are operated by nationals of other countries, including Germans. Because of the continued sensitivity of the German question, this would strain NATO cohesion during a crisis. The provocative nature of the QRA system, its high vulnerability, its inconsistency with a dissuasion strategy, and its likely effects on NATO cohesion argue against its retention. Yet, if all aircraft that could carry nuclear weapons were removed, NATO ground forces would lose essential tactical air support.

QRAs Distinguished from Tactical Air. An effective NATO defense requires tactical air support. One aspect of tactical air support involves actions designed to reduce WTO tactical air support. Thus, one would expect NATO's targeting plans to include WTO airfields, a mission for which QRAs (and also Pershings) are admirably suited. It is likely that the heavy price involved in not targeting WTO airfields with QRAs —a mission involving large-scale collateral damage in Eastern Europe—

would be justified by the gains resulting from dissuasion. If other aircraft are not distinguishable from QRAs because all, including helicopters, could carry nuclear bombs, the removal of all aircraft to achieve dissuasion would be a very high price indeed. However, the situation is actually much more favorable than this paragraph suggests. A clear distinction can be made between QRAs and tactical aircraft, and there are other means of reducing WTO tactical air support.

Only a particular class of aircraft is specifically designated for strategic nuclear missions. The Soviet posture at SALT accepts this restrictive designation. This might be good enough, but in addition, there are good military reasons for a distinction. These are the only aircraft that can carry strategic nuclear weapons to the Soviet Union and return without refuelling. If the QRAs are removed, changes in the visible characteristics of tactical aircraft—for instance, configuration and bomb racks—could provide assurance that no aircraft remaining on the central front have QRA capabilities. Thus, removal or rebasing of the QRAs need not be inconsistent with those tactical air missions that are highly important for successful ground operations. Even the strategic nuclear bomb dumps can be removed as an assurance that tactical aircraft cannot engage in one-way strategic strikes against WTO allies of the Soviet Union. The cost of this would be small to NATO.

If NATO is determined to blunt the tactical air power of the Soviet Union, it instead can invest in SAM D (surface-to-air missiles), which very likely would provide a highly effective air defense. This is a particularly effective alternative because so many of the WTO airfields are in the Soviet Union, and thus, constitute targets that the United States could not hit with nuclear weapons without legitimating nuclear attacks on the continental United States. Moreover, as WTO airfields in Eastern Europe are highly dispersed, and as Soviet planes are quickly transferable to them from the Soviet Union, the WTO fields are far less attractive targets than the fields used by the U.S. tactical air force in Europe. If the nuclear targeting of WTO airfields should come to be considered essential in a war, this mission can be transferred to MIRVed Polaris/Poseidon submarine-borne ballistic missiles. As this targeting mission would involve little collateral damage in Eastern Europe, it would be consistent with dissuasion and would have the additional advantage of credibly relating a use of the American strategic nuclear force to NATO defense.

61

Rebasing QRAs. QRAs need not be removed entirely from the NATO arsenal of weapons. They could be rebased in a sanctuary in England or the United States and returned to the continent if needed. If the Soviet Union did not know when they would return or at which airfields they would land, whether military or civilian, whether permanent or temporary, their chances of survival and active participation in war, if needed later, would be better than if retained in their current locations. Moreover, the removal of weapons systems associated with provocative possibilities legitimately can be viewed as a step toward détente. In this sense, the proposal is consistent with President Nixon's call for an era of negotiations.

The Argument against Removal and Rebasing. The primary argument for retaining QRAs in central Europe is that they are the American nuclear hostage to Europe. This argument reveals a lack of confidence in the credibility of the American strategic deterrent. If Germans, for instance, really believed that the strategic deterrent would be used in their defense, they would not need their finger on the trigger of this extremely vulnerable and provocative hostage.

It is the very provocative character of the QRA system that produces the trigger effect—in particular, the American control on the Germans may not be that clear to the U.S.S.R. or that important, in view of the vulnerability of the QRA, even if control is relatively clear. To the extent that German reliance on the finger-on-the-trigger argument depends upon this exceptionally provocative character of the weapons system, rebasing must be compensated for by a more credible linkage of the American deterrent to the defense of Western Europe. (This could be done by the Polaris/Poseidon targetting that will be explained later in this chapter.) However, to the extent that direct German control of weapons systems carrying nuclear weapons is the essential element as far as the Germans are concerned—even if the warheads are under ultimate American control—rebasing, especially in the continental United States where the likelihood of Soviet preemption is minimal, would continue to meet this need. In this case, the Germans would have a far more assured use of the system than under current conditions, for the survivability of the QRA would be correspondingly higher.

One other possible objection by Germans to the rebasing of the QRAs is that rebasing might reduce their diplomatic influence in situations involving important German interests that were not of crisis proportion. This possible objection may be too sophisticated. If the German QRAs are rebased, the Germans would still retain on German soil all their tactical aircraft that cannot reach the Soviet Union and return. Even if the QRAs were retained, the Germans would not control their nuclear warheads. Any attempt by the Germans, whether blatant or subtle, to use control of the QRAs for purposes of pressure would likely raise the fear that they might somehow obtain the warheads. They might gain some marginal diplomatic mileage from this but they would probably lose far more, for they would strain their alliance relations with their West European allies and with the United States. Even if Germany were to hope unwisely that it could trade on the fear that it might develop an independent policy unless it was supported by NATO allies, this hope would not be increased by the retention of German QRAs on German soil. The requirement of the QRAs for American warheads would emphasize German dependence on the United States at the same time that German use of the QRAs for leverage alienated its allies.

On the other hand, rebasing the QRAs would establish a German claim on allied support. It would remove German fears concerning the pressures that might be placed upon them to remove the QRAs under crisis conditions. And Germany would gain the subtle leverage that it could unilaterally bring the German QRAs back to German soil if it was left without support by its allies. Moreover, with the QRAs rebased, Germany would gain the advantage of a credible allied war-fighting plan. Yet, it would not possess so potent an independent force that it would frighten the French into a more independent policy or undermine the reasons for retention of American forces in Germany.

There is reason to believe that those Germans who desire the trigger effect of the QRA do so only for its deterrence value, for with the failure of deterrence, QRA installations likely would invite nuclear attacks in the middle-kiloton or higher range, with consequent enormous collateral damage in West Germany. In a crisis escalating out of control, or at least having the appearance of doing so, the QRAs likely would weaken German resolve during crisis bargaining and would produce demands for their removal. Such demands, whether successful or not, would be evidence of a lack of resolution in Germany and in NATO. On the other hand, voluntary withdrawal of the QRAs and the Pershings during a noncrisis period in the context of strategic plans designed to improve NATO performance levels would be a sign of strength.

Pershings, QRAs, and Nuclear Firebreaks

Many doubt that distinctions can be drawn in combat between levels of use of nuclear weapons. Some make a broad distinction between strategic and tactical nuclear weapons. All serious analysts hope that this dispute will never have empirical relevance. If, however, a decision is made to use nuclear weapons in combat, it is desirable to preserve postures that enhance the prospects for a firebreak between levels of use, and that enhance intrawar deterrence.

Some strategists advocate the use of subkiloton nuclear weapons in close ground support operations if NATO is outmatched conventionally in Europe. These subkiloton weapons, which have no counterpart in the WTO weapons systems as yet, produce minimal collateral damage. Unlike the Pershings, or even the shorter-range, lower-payload Sergeant missile, these subkiloton nuclear weapons can be directed effectively at divisional and lower level targets.

First use of nuclear weapons by NATO runs the risk of a Soviet nuclear response. However, in the absence of Pershings and QRAs, there are almost no targets—with the possible exception of some airfields —against which the large Soviet tactical nuclear weapons could be used, unless the Soviet Union decided to hit cities, and that would be a very serious and drastic escalation. It is difficult to see what incentive the Soviet Union would have to do this, for such a move would increase the probability that its own cities would become targets. Thus, removal of the QRAs, Pershings and Sergeants would enhance the prospects for a firebreak. If, however, Pershings and QRAs are present, there would be no obvious firebreak between subkiloton weapons and weapons producing major collateral damage, for the QRAs and relatively stationary Pershings are obvious targets in a war that is already nuclear in a tactical sense, whereas the highly mobile Lance missile is extremely difficult to target. This advantage of removing the QRAs and Pershings (maintaining a nuclear firebreak) is marginal and uncertain, but it is highly important to enhance whatever prospect there may be of a firebreak.

The Dissuasion Strategy

WTO Dissuasion Distinguished from WTO Disruption. The dissuasion strategy must be distinguished from a strategy designed to undermine the Warsaw Pact in peacetime. Such a strategy would fail for a number of reasons. The WTO regimes are dependent upon the existence of a strong Soviet Union. Except in Bulgaria, which has a history of great friendship for the Soviet Union, and in Rumania, where the regime has considerable support because of its independence, the WTO regimes have only limited popularity and are accepted by the local populations largely because of fear of Soviet intervention. Thus, measures designed to force a rupture between the Soviet Union and the other members of the pact would be contrary to the interests of the current regimes. In addition, these regimes must have little doubt concerning the Soviet response if they volunteer to neutralize themselves in peacetime. The dissuasion strategy is designed to avoid exploitation of any possible cleavage in the WTO except in case of a Soviet aggressive war in the NATO area.

The Dissuasion Concept. The dissuasion concept operates only in case of a Russian attack against the NATO area, but the strategy has implications for peacetime crises. The dissuasion concept distinguishes between Eastern Europe and the Soviet Union as target areas. Under this concept, NATO would deliberately avoid the use of weapons systems that would produce large amounts of collateral damage in Eastern Europe or that would do grievous injury to the East European economies and social and political infrastructures. For example, NATO would attack only those transportation facilities that are used by Soviet attacking forces. Conventional weapons would be used, if possible, and damage that would have long-term effects would be minimized. However, these restrictions would be observed only as long as the WTO armies refrained from cooperation in the Soviet attack. Cooperation would be defined as direct engagement in attacks, the holding of static positions in Soviet lines that forced a diversion of NATO manpower, interference with NATO flanking actions in the area of attack, or the giving of active support to Soviet behind-the-lines operations. (Mobilization for defense, but not in the vicinity of the NATO/WTO boundary, would not be considered grounds for lifting the restrictions.)

WTO members would not be asked to refuse permission to Soviet troops to use their territories for attack or to interfere with Soviet utilization of local supplies or logistic facilities. This is because WTO regimes would expect that actions directly hostile to the Soviet Union would be met by the immediate use of force. If NATO asked them to interfere with Soviet war measures, it would place them in a dreadful dilemma. On the other hand, the Soviet Union would have no good riposte to their merely remaining passive, for Soviet attempts to coerce the WTO regimes into providing military support would interfere with its military activities against NATO.

In the event East European members of WTO engaged in any of the interdicted activities, after population warning to permit the local populations to avoid attack zones, NATO would begin with small attacks upon their economic infrastructures. If this warning were not heeded, and if the regimes did not refrain from the interdicted activities within a reasonable period of time, their economic infrastructures would be destroyed if necessary. Such attacks would be clearly distinguished from threats against the Soviet Union.

The fact that a Soviet effort to coerce WTO military support would subject WTO regimes to damage the Soviet regime did not risk—at least immediately—would be viewed by these regimes as a moral outrage. They would risk the small degree of domestic consensus they have by participating in such an attack. This would raise even higher the military cost of attempted Soviet coercion. This strategy does not hold the WTO regimes hostage to Soviet decisions, for under these conditions, they reasonably can be expected to successfully resist Soviet calls for their active support in aggressive war.

The dissuasion strategy would ease the position of the Eastern European nations. Although it increases the likelihood of an actual use of nuclear weapons against the Eastern European nations if war breaks out and if they participate, current strategies make this risk high in any event, as the primary NATO targetting—including nuclear—lies in their territories. The dissuasion strategy removes those weapons that do the greatest collateral damage, and provides the Eastern European members of the WTO with a greater opportunity to avoid participation in war—and thus to avoid damage—and to resist Soviet decisions either to escalate crises or to begin a war. The fact of Soviet organizational control within the Warsaw Treaty Organization forces is largely irrelevant to this argument.

The extent of the control makes manifest Soviet lack of confidence in its WTO partners. However, paper control is most unlikely to be exerted successfully against national governments that are unwilling to have their troops move under the conditions of the dissuasion strategy. The patent reluctance of its Eastern European partners to agree to the escalation of crises would reduce the coercive bargaining power of the

Soviet Union during crises, and increase the confidence of Western European nations in resisting objectionable Soviet demands. The dissuasion strategy provides the Eastern European partners of the Soviet Union with a reasonable method of resisting aggressive Soviet demands without rupturing the Warsaw Treaty Organization. At the same time it satisfies their security interests by eliminating the most provocative weapons systems from the theater and by replacing them with extra-theater weapons that are more precise and that involve far less collateral damage.

Dissuasion will confer numerous benefits upon all European nations —East and West—who prefer peace, détente, and crisis management to instability in Europe. Dissuasion is a concept which, applied to NATO strategy, is designed to rectify the initial offensive advantage of the WTO in the European theater. It is consistent with the removal from the European theater of weapons that are provocative in a crisis and escalatory in a war. It links the U.S. deterrent to the defense of Europe more credibly than current strategies. It is based on symmetrical principles that reinforce détente and improve the climate for peaceful change. It poses no threat to either alliance system in peace. However, the incentive structure it creates will tend to disrupt the alliance stability of NATO or the WTO if either attempts to escalate a crisis deliberately or to exploit an incident militarily rather than to terminate the incident. It, thus, symmetrically reinforces motivations to dampen crises and to terminate military incidents. It provides the nations of WTO and of NATO opportunities to insulate themselves from the provocative acts of their allies. It is credible to the U.S.S.R. and its WTO allies because current Soviet strategy provides for the avoidance of nuclear targets in the United States but for the use of nuclear weapons in Western Europe. Thus, they are disposed to believe that the U.S. strategy is symmetrical. The WTO allies of the Soviet Union have as much incentive to cooperate with dissuasion as the NATO allies of the United States do under similar circumstances.

Dissuasion and a Credible Deterrent. If the WTO members were nonetheless to join in an attack against the NATO area, the threatened punishment would be initiated. An effort would be made to avoid nuclear weapons. However, if they were required, the Polaris/Poseidon fleet would be used. The United States could employ either those vessels under control of SACEUR (Supreme Allied Commander Europe), to

67

assure Europeans that NATO-assigned weapons systems are available, or it could use Polaris/Poseidon vessels not linked to NATO to decrease the responsibility of our NATO partners for nuclear actions. The employment of the American deterrent in this mission would be highly credible, for the Soviet Union could strike at the continental U.S. only by placing its own homeland at risk. With population warning, damage to humans would be limited because of the small warhead size of the mission force.

It is important to note that the dissuasion strategy does not decouple the American strategic system from deterrence of the Soviet Union. To the extent that the members of NATO rely upon the ambiguous nature of this type of deterrence and upon the presence of American forces as hostages—a threat that depends on a small probability of a devastating event—the Soviet Union cannot exclude the possibility that the United States may decide to use its nuclear weapons against its homeland. The dissuasion strategy, however, does perform a symbolic decoupling between attacks in Eastern Europe and on the Soviet Union. This immensely increases the probability of employment against Eastern European nations—if war occurs and if they participate in it—without substantially decreasing the threat against the Soviet Union. The strategy also enhances the salience of the British and French nuclear forces. Moreover, because the strategy provides a credible war-fighting capability, it reduces the temptation to the United States, whose citizens place little value on the hostage argument, to allow reductions in American NATO forces precisely because they would now be relevant to NATO's war-fighting capability. Thus, by increasing the likelihood that reductions in American ground forces would be minimal, the strategy also enhances the hostage value of American forces, and serves this purpose better than current strategic conceptions.

Crisis Stability. Many Europeans assert that they depend upon the ambiguous nature of the American deterrent threat. The assumption is that a very small probability of a devastating result will serve to deter the Soviet Union from an attack upon Western Europe. This is not an entirely unreasonable assumption, but it does misstate the nature of the problem to some extent. Even if it is true, and this is surely less than certain, that the ambiguous nature of the American threat will serve to deter an actual Soviet attack, it does not follow that the same kind of ambiguous threat will deter the initiation of a crisis. In the first place, a crisis may occur independently of the wills of the major governments as a consequence of events beyond their control. In the second place, the Soviet Union might initiate a crisis with the intention of stopping short of war if it believed it could obtain some major advantage from this. Unfortunately, NATO could not be sure of Soviet intentions. During the crisis the western European members of NATO would come face-to-face with their own reluctance to employ a suicidal strategy, and thus, with the lack of credibility of their strategic plan. This may not be a major risk during a period of détente in which the interest of the Soviet Union in avoiding a crisis in Western Europe is quite high. It would be extremely hazardous to assume that such conditions will persist indefinitely, although one hopes for an improvement rather than a worsening of the present situation.

The dissuasion strategy would provide a more credible plan for crisis management for a number of reasons. Because of its symbolic decoupling of an attack upon Eastern Europe from an immediate attack upon the Soviet Union, it would make such a use of the American deterrent force quite credible. Because this threat would be credible, the strategy would impinge on the cohesion of the Warsaw Treaty Organization in only those situations in which the Soviet Union attempted to use the organization for aggressive purposes. This would reduce the credibility of the Soviet threat and weaken Soviet bargaining power during such an induced crisis. In addition, as the dissuasion strategy would improve the war-fighting capability of NATO, it would further decrease Soviet bargaining power during an induced crisis.

Because the cohesion and credibility of NATO would be improved, the coupling of the American deterrent to a potential attack upon the Soviet Union would be increased. Although this may seem paradoxical at first sight, it is really a quite natural development. If the war-fighting capability of NATO is weak, and if the threat is intended primarily as a deterrent rather than as an actual element in a war, then the Soviet Union can hope to expose it as a bluff during a crisis. If, however, the position of NATO is sufficiently strong to maintain its will and cohesion during the crisis period, then the crisis could not easily be used to decouple the American deterrent threat prior to an actual outbreak of hostilities. In such circumstances, the Soviet Union would find it most difficult to work upon the will of either the United States or the Western European members of NATO to encourage a demand for decoupling in order to avoid either provocation or the consequences of actual use of the deterrent. However, if war were to break out, the Soviet Union would not be able to exclude the possibility that the deterrent might be used during the war, and thus, the deterrent effect against the Soviet Union is actually increased by the decoupling of Eastern Europe from the Soviet Union in a staged process of use during war.

Publication of Dissuasion. Dissuasion might be adopted in a number of ways. If adopted by NATO, it could become known by means of newspaper reports of NATO discussions. Thus, even in this case, an explicit declaration would be unnecessary. On the other hand, some of our NATO partners might regard discussion of dissuasion as an incentive to the Soviet Union either to undermine détente or to engage in propaganda directed to the Western publics to the effect that dissuasion threatened détente. The West German policy of *Ostpolitik* might be particularly vulnerable to this type of ploy. To avoid this, the United States might adopt a policy of dissuasion tacitly, letting the policy become known by means of internal discussion and by force dispositions consonant with it, some of which have been suggested in this book. Of course, it would be inappropriate not to discuss the strategy with our allies, but it could be done on a more private basis if this choice were made. In this sense, there might not be any actual formal adoption of dissuasion, but the Eastern European states nonetheless would become aware of its likelihood in the event of an outbreak of war. Thus, it would have much the same effect upon the political processes preceding a decision to attack, or even more important, to escalate a crisis, as a more formal adoption of dissuasion.

It should be made clear that dissuasion is not designed to produce an asymmetrical Western advantage. The possibility of Soviet adoption of a similar strategy in the case of a West European attack, with American cooperation, upon Eastern Europe should be recognized. Moreover, the emphasis should be upon controlling the course of military disputes. Thus, definitions of aggression would be beside the point. Or, to put it another way, the aggressor would not necessarily be the state that initiated the hostilities but the state that continued them by intrusions into the territory of the other bloc.

Dissuasion, therefore, puts its emphasis upon the termination of hostility and places the onus upon those states that do not cooperate to this end. In this sense, although dissuasion does not imply any legal

70

or formal recognition of the status quo in Europe, it does respond to all those proposals that, in one form or another, place emphasis upon the avoidance of the use of force in Europe. Dissuasion broadens this consideration, however, by recognizing that if, for some unforeseen reason, force should be resorted to, the goal would then become the termination of hostilities upon the basis of the status quo ante. Thus, it emphasizes the same principle, namely, that force should not be used to change the status quo in Europe.

Dissuasion and WTO Decision Making

It would be a mistake to view the dissuasion strategy solely from the standpoint of its impact upon the actual course of battle. It is designed to diminish the likelihood of decisions to escalate crises to a level at which military operations come into consideration.

If one examines the situation before the Warsaw Pact powers attacked Czechoslovakia in 1968, one notices extensive discussions among the Soviet Union and the other Warsaw Pact members as well as negotiations between them and the Czechoslovaks. In part, this was probably related to a Soviet effort for political/moral reasons to find some rationale that would win the "willing" cooperation of other pact members to military operations. The Soviet Union could have carried out the attack entirely by itself, although it would have had to use WTO territory and logistics. The WTO members would hardly have resisted unilateral Soviet action. Yet, given the obvious difficulties of the debate within the Soviet Union, it is not clear that it could have brought itself to the decision to attack in the absence of support from at least some of the other members of the Warsaw Pact.

Perhaps one might argue that the political/moral situation would be different in the event of a Soviet attack on Western Europe. In a venture of this magnitude, perhaps it might be argued that the Soviet Union would be less concerned with political/moral consequences than with the opportunity to make a major change in the structure of world politics. However, this assumes the character of the Soviet decision-making process to be monolithic. Surely some within the Politburo would argue for consultations with other pact members; even some in the military might support such consultation because of the need for secure logistic lines. The very process of consultation in a venture of this magnitude would emphasize differences of interests between the Soviet

71

Union and the other members of the Warsaw Pact. Such discussions might become threatening to the cohesiveness of the WTO, even in the absence of a definite decision to attack, and thus, serve as a barrier to escalatory measures that begin to carry the threat of a military outbreak. The dissuasion strategy would place pressure on the Soviet Union to search for means of accommodation with the Western powers in order to avoid cleavages within the Warsaw Pact.

Apart from the direct, but perhaps slight, influence other Warsaw Pact members might have upon the Soviet decision process, they might have a major indirect impact insofar as they give ammunition to those members of the Politburo opposed to escalatory steps. This again emphasizes the importance of the intervening variable in attack situations.

We are not trying to make the case for dissuasion too strong. We do not argue that the Soviet Union necessarily could be deterred from attack or that the dissuasion strategy necessarily would work. Dissuasion, however, has three persuasive merits: it would reduce the likelihood of a decision to attack; it likely would reduce the war-fighting capability of the attacking forces if the decision to attack were made; and it likely would delay the decision to attack long enough for NATO's superior long-range mobilization capabilities to be brought into play, if in the meantime, NATO made use of its opportunities.

In the latter case, the troops need not be brought to the central front. If, as the dissuasion strategy provides, provocative weapons systems are removed from the central front, the newly mobilized troops and their equipment might be sent to prepared bases in England, where they would constitute no immediate threat to the defensive capabilities of the Warsaw Pact powers. Furthermore, because these factors would increase confidence in NATO, alliance cohesion would be improved and this also would affect the WTO decision process adversely with respect to war decisions.

A Soviet Dissuasion Strategy?

Could the dissuasion strategy be turned around and used by the Soviet Union? Soviet forces make a far greater comparative contribution to Warsaw Pact potential than United States forces do to NATO's. Could not the Soviet Union dissuade the West European members of NATO from participating in defensive operations?

For instance, consider a Soviet nuclear threat against France or Great Britain designed to inhibit the cooperation of one or the other with German defense. This threat might work, but note carefully that it is of a different order from the American threat against Eastern Europe under the dissuasion strategy. The United States would not ask any of the East European states to stand by while it made an effort to change the status quo in the Warsaw Pact area. Thus, although recognizing that events not fully under control may constitute a threat to security in the Warsaw Pact, the United States would not by any direct action of its own threaten to reduce the security of the Soviet Union or of the other members of the Warsaw Pact. Even defeat of an attack, depending upon how tenaciously the Soviet Union presses its military operations before agreeing to negotiations, would not interfere in any major way with the ability of the Soviet Union to protect the existing regimes in East Europe.

On the other hand, if one of the NATO regimes allows itself to be dissuaded from opposing a major change in the status quo in the NATO area, it would weaken in a major way its own national security. If the assurance of the NATO alliance partners is weaker than that of the WTO states, or if the NATO members are less afraid of American retaliation— or more afraid of Soviet retaliation—they may allow themselves to be dissuaded from defense. However, if this is the case, the Soviet Union could employ this threat against them—and would find it easier to do so, for it would retain the aid of its allies—in the absence of a NATO dissuasion strategy. Indeed, if the Soviet Union ever decided to go to war in the NATO area, it is not unlikely that it would make such threats either explicitly or implicitly.

Could the Soviet Union hope to dissuade the United States from employing its dissuasion strategy by threatening the NATO partners of the United States? This also might work, for obviously the U.S. would be concerned about the fate of its alliance partners. However, the Soviet Union would be threatening a target area, namely the American alliance partners in NATO, that did not control the threat being used against the East Europeans. If the Soviet Union carried out such a threat, it would run a serious risk that the United States would respond by an attack directly against the Soviet Union, or that the United States would return the QRAs for use by the threatened countries or employ the quick-transfer capability discussed below.

Could the Soviet Union threaten to hit the United States with nuclear weapons if American nuclear weapons were transferred to

Germany during war? The very same threat could be made against the United States with respect to its use of either strategic or tactical nuclear weapons. The threat could also be made to deter the United States from a conventional defense of West Germany. For the Soviet Union to enforce the threat by hitting the United States would be to subject itself to the American as well as to a West German deterrent system. This is possible, but it hardly seems likely. In short, although the dissuasion strategy does not eliminate the alliance and domestic political difficulties affecting pluralistic, democratic systems, it minimizes them by using those asymmetries that favor NATO in that case in which the Soviet Union attacks it.

The Quick-Transfer Capability

What of the case where dissuasion and conventional defense—and *a fortiori* deterrence—have failed? The deterrent could then be used, but it would lead only to mutual destruction. That this is desired by many Europeans and Americans is doubtful. There is one other possible solution to this problem, a solution that because of its controversial nature is not practicable but which the author believes would increase deterrence if adopted: a quick-transfer capability.

With a quick-transfer capability, in the event that war occurs and conventional defense fails, the United States would deliver to the victim of the attack a specified number of Polaris/Poseidon submarines for which European national crews have been trained in advance. Some might view this quick-transfer capability as a violation of the nuclear nonproliferation treaty. This is quite wrong, for the treaty specifically excludes circumstances where vital national interests are involved. In fact, however, the quick-transfer capability is a step away from, rather than a step toward, nuclear proliferation.

In the case of West Germany, a specific response tailored to her particular circumstances is warranted. The objections of the Soviet Union and of the West European powers to German nuclearization have ostensible weight primarily because of Germany's past history. Although the Soviet use of this argument is probably primarily tactical, the claim that it fears a revanchist German government that might use these weapons appeals to certain publics in the West. (These expressed fears, which treat Germany as a permanent pariah nation, are more likely to bring about the feared nationalistic German policies than is German nuclearization—particularly as subsequent generations of young Germans may view this policy as irrationally discriminatory and insulting, and may rightly feel no personal responsibility for past German history.) However, those who fear a future nuclearization of Germany logically should be reassured by a quick-transfer capability, for it removes most of the incentive for German nuclearization. The argument for a German nuclear force is related, as was the Gaullist argument for French nuclearization, to the relatively low credibility of the American deterrent. The German case is strengthened by the nonexistence of a European nuclear system in which there is German participation. To the extent that one believes that Germany would be extremely unlikely to develop an independent nuclear force in peacetime except as a last resort, the quick-transfer capability removes the potential need to make that decision. In the event that Germany becomes the battle area and that conventional defense cannot prevent Soviet forces from making strong incursions into West Germany, Germany will have available to it on its demand—if the quick-transfer capability is achieved—a nuclear force capable of destroying the major Soviet cities.

From a German point of view, this quick-transfer nuclear force probably would have one striking advantage over an independent nuclear force. Although such an arrangement would not possess the prestige value of the French nuclear force, Germany would be able to avoid the danger of peacetime possession of such a force, namely, that possession would precipitate a serious crisis in peacetime. The option would arise only if Germany were losing a major war. Unless it chose to surrender, the only threat the Soviet Union would have against its use of the quick-transfer option would be that of a nuclear attack. However, the Soviet Union could carry out this threat against a secondary member of the NATO alliance only at the risk of losing Moscow and Leningrad—cities which are far more important to it than are any two equivalent cities to the United States—as well as other major population centers. Such a quick-transfer capability would thus have enormous deterrence value, and at the same time, would constitute a barrier to the proliferation of nuclear systems—an argument that might appeal to those who oppose proliferation.

As the Germans would never actually be in physical possession of armed nuclear submarines except in wartime if the quick-transfer policy is adopted, the policy poses no threat to the Soviet Union—and actually removes a potential threat—unless it has some future intention of attacking Germany. This is hardly an argument that it could make public in peacetime, although it might make less logical but more appealing arguments against the proposal. The French or British would not be entirely happy with the thought of a potential German force, even in wartime. However, their opposition would be equivalent to arguing that if a NATO conventional defense of Germany failed and if the United States, Great Britain, and France were individually and collectively unwilling to use their nuclear weapons to support Germany, it should surrender.

The quick-transfer capability is also a potential solution to a crisis in Yugoslavia after Tito's death or to trouble elsewhere on the southern flank of NATO. The knowledge that, if attacked, the Yugoslavs, the Greeks, or the Turks would receive one or more Polaris/Poseidon submarines would have enormous deterrence value. Of course, the Yugoslavs are such renowned fighters that even an airlift capability for conventional weapons to the mountain regions of Yugoslavia might be sufficient protection.

Relations with the Yugoslavs are apparently a matter of dispute in the Soviet Union. On the one hand, the Russians are reported to finance the *Ustachi,* a fascist emigré organization headquartered in West Germany that engages in terroristic actions. The recent agreement between the Yugoslavs and the Soviet Union, which states the right of each to proceed to socialism along its own path, may contain a hidden joker. If the Russians ever determine that the Yugoslav path is no longer socialistic, then presumably the Brezhnev Doctrine would apply. On the other hand, the measures of détente the Soviet Union has been taking in coordination with the United States would seem to preclude such direct intervention, as apparently would the Nixon-Brezhnev Moscow meeting. Yet, even if unlikely, a Soviet takeover of an area now defined as outside of the Soviet sphere of influence in Europe would make for extremely depressing prospects for both the central and southern flanks of NATO. In particular, pressures upon the Italians might become quite heavy, thus threatening to turn the Mediterranean into a Russian lake, with obvious consequences for the entire Middle East. A strategy capable of deterring or of defeating such intervention, even if relatively unlikely, surely has much to recommend it.

In the absence of a quick-transfer capability, dissuasion provides a credible war-fighting strategy for the central front, with weaknesses remaining primarily in the Mediterranean and on the northern flanks of

NATO. Some might advocate the use of the quick-transfer option only on the northern and southern flanks to avoid sensitivities on the German question. This would be a mistake. Such an obvious case of discrimination would threaten alliance cohesion on the central front.

The quick-transfer capability deliberately is a detachable part of the dissuasion strategy. Although this writer considers it a highly desirable aspect of the strategy, not unlikely political objections by West European countries could preclude its adoption. Some of the objections to a potential nuclear arming of Germany are so strong that serious discussion of it might even prove divisive for this reason. The English, the low countries, and the Scandinavian countries retain sensitivities resulting from the Second World War, although important generational changes have occurred. The French attitude toward the German force is much like the attitude of the Kennedy administration toward de Gaulle's force. Although the French attitudes may suffer from moral, political, and strategic blindness in the same way as did earlier American attitudes to France, they exist. In Germany, the only important support for any form of German control over nuclear weapons now comes from the Christian Socialist Union, with its strength concentrated in Bavaria. Chancellor Brandt would resist such an idea at the present time for a number of reasons. Apparently he has strong moral inhibitions on the subject of nuclear weapons for Germany. If he moved in that direction, he would infuriate the strong left wing within the German Socialist party, particularly its youth wing. Such a move might well threaten Chancellor Brandt's policy of *Ostpolitik* and injure détente. It would likely subject him to Soviet pressure and might isolate Germany politically. However, a collapse of *Ostpolitik* and of détente might shift attitudes on a quick-transfer capability in a short period of time. Therefore, under current conditions, it must be admitted that it is not a realistic suggestion. On the other hand, contingency plans related to a quick-transfer project might make excellent military and political sense.

Dissuasion and . . .

Allied Force Contributions. The dissuasion strategy emphasizes force postures and missions better adapted to the situations of the European members of NATO than current force postures and missions, for instance, tactical air defense as opposed to strategic nuclear air missions. By increasing the range of credible options available to our NATO partners, the dissuasion strategy improves the ways in which they can participate meaningfully in NATO planning. By reducing their dependence upon the ultimate sanction of massive retaliation, it reduces the extent to which they are clients of the American nuclear option.

In addition, the assignment of the major strategic targetting in the dissuasion strategy to the Polaris/Poseidon force increases the salience of the British and French submarine contributions to theater nuclear forces. The QRAs are relatively identifiable. Missiles launched from English or French Polaris submarines are far more difficult to identify. Thus, they could be used to hit East European, or even Soviet, targets, and the Soviet Union would not know against whom to respond. The fact that it knew it might be faced with this dilemma would be an additional deterrent to the Soviet Union. Given the overwhelming importance of the two cities of Moscow and Leningrad to the Soviet Union, these would be "hostage" to any of the allied submarine forces. Yet specific Soviet deterrence of submarine strikes against them would be limited because of the identification problem.

Alliance Assurance. By removing the QRAs and the Pershings, the attractive and provocative targets that Soviet short-range missiles are deployed to hit would be gone from West European countries. As a consequence, unless the Soviet Union for some presently unexplainable reason decides on a punishment strategy that strikes at population, these countries would receive less collateral damage in a war that escalated to the nuclear level. Thus, the likelihood that their will would weaken during a crisis is reduced if these aspects of the strategy are adopted. Because the dissuasion strategy would provide a greater war-fighting capability, deter Soviet attack, and dissuade participation by Warsaw Pact members, war would appear less likely, the range of Soviet options less deadly, the counter-responses to Soviet moves more credible, and the possibility of intrawar deterrence greater. The importance of this degree of alliance reassurance can hardly be overstated.

The greatest threat to NATO lies not in the probability of Soviet attack but in the perception by many Europeans that such an attack either could not be defeated or that it would be too damaging. West Europeans have resisted adequate conventional forces for economic and partly for internal political reasons. But they have also resisted them for fear that seemingly adequate conventional forces would impair employment of the American strategic deterrent on their behalf. They have feared flexible response because it seemed to imply a reduction in the American willingness to employ the deterrent. Yet their preference for massive retaliation has not been a preference for its employment but only for its deterrence value. To the extent that these attitudes have had military and political consequences for the alliance, they have marginally reduced the willingness of the European members to support the conventional war-fighting capability of NATO. Whether they have really purchased any additional deterrence is open to serious question, for a strategy that no one would be willing to employ has little credibility in a crisis. Moreover, if one is in such a crisis and has only deterrence to rely on, there would be a natural temptation to overvalue Soviet political offers, to seek to avoid provocative positions that might increase the risk of war, and to search for measures of accommodation even though these might weaken the interests of the members of NATO. Under contemporary benign circumstances, these conditions are not genuinely dangerous. Under future adverse circumstances, they might lead to the Finlandization of West Europe through accommodation. Because the dissuasion strategy would significantly improve the war-fighting capability of NATO and credibly links the American deterrent to this capability, there is a significant increase in deterrence of the Soviet Union. At the same time, because it removes provocative weapons systems from the central front it is consistent with conciliation between the two blocs, the negotiation of differences, crisis dampening, and balanced arms reductions.

United States Defense Costs. The reformulation of missions permitted by the dissuasion strategy would permit major reductions in costs, reaching at least into the hundreds of millions of dollars, and perhaps much higher. The rebasing of the QRAs would permit a reduction in American forces of at least the 50,000 that the Mansfield plan requires. However, in the absence of the credible war-fighting capability provided by the dissuasion strategy, there would be no reason to reject continued cuts in the American forces in Europe. If the armed forces cannot play a credible war-fighting role—and if their mission is primarily that of symbolic hostages—the actual number of troops is not of great significance (although the fact of reductions may be). If, however, after the initial reductions the troops remaining in Western Europe are required within the framework of a credible war-fighting plan, resistance to further cuts would be strengthened.

Morality. No war is entirely moral, and consequently, no strategy, however necessary or justified, is entirely moral. However, by removing weapons systems that produce enormous collateral damage the dissuasion strategy would improve NATO's moral position. If the United States is forced to carry out the threat that provides the rationale for dissuasion of the WTO, that would have a very adverse effect upon human life as a consequence of destruction of the economic infrastructure. This is far preferable to the alternatives, including present strategic targeting, and the means of avoiding this result are within the possession of the governments and even, to some extent, of the peoples of East Europe. The effects of the strategy would not be visited upon them at once. There would be several demonstrations and they would have several clear chances to avoid these results. Moreover, they would be able to avoid this result—and even in extreme form, it is far less deadly than the implications of current strategy—in a way that does not place them upon the horns of a deadly dilemma. This should be fully apparent to the populations in those countries, and their governments will be aware that their peoples know this.

The moderate character of the threat which would be invoked by the dissuasion strategy would increase its deterrence value, both by increasing U.S. willingness to employ it and by improving the means for East European governments to avoid participation in war. The heaviest moral and political pressures would be placed upon these regimes to avoid punishment. The Soviet Union would be placed in an exceptionally awkward, if not actually untenable, position if it attempted to coerce WTO compliance with plans for aggressive war.

If, at the same time, NATO reasonably attempted to negotiate the real problems that give rise to the crisis—but from a position of political, military, and moral strength—the prospects for the continued independence and autonomy of its members would be exceptionally good. What at present appears to be a quite weak position would have been turned into a quite strong one. This could make its effects felt in many other parts of the world and with respect to many other important issues concerning the structure and tone of world politics.

Balanced Force Reductions. The dissuasion strategy is obviously compatible with moves toward mutual balanced force reductions, and though it is not dependent on them, it is important, of course, that reductions lead to increased security and stability in Europe. In this respect, it would be helpful if the Soviet Union eliminated or reduced its intermediate-range (IRBM) and medium-range (MRBM) ballistic missile forces in response to NATO's removal of Pershings and QRAs. It should also remove from Eastern Europe its heavier short-range ballistic missiles (SRBMs), the warheads of which would produce considerable collateral damage. The American Sergeant missiles could be retained for partial trading off against the Soviet SRBMs, although it is possible that NATO might remove these systems unilaterally. However, a Soviet refusal to reciprocate, given the relative lack of utility of its SRBMs, IRBMs, and MRBMs, except against population, would raise questions concerning its good faith.

In general, the changes that are made should be considered primarily from the standpoint of stability. Thus, for instance, it might be desirable to mutually improve defensive fortifications but to reduce the number of tank and heavy armored divisions, or rapid mobile units, in the nations on the borders between the two blocs. The size of actual troop reductions should be strictly related to different mobilization capabilities. Thus, for instance, too great a reduction in central Europe by both sides might permit the initial 30-day mobilization advantage of the Soviet Union to produce a winning capability during a crisis. Whether political and military factors would permit the Western powers to remove subkiloton nuclear weapons and demolition mines from their arsenals in the contact areas requires detailed analysis.

The Soviet Union has been vacillating on the subject of mutual balanced force reductions (MBFR). In any event, if it does discuss this issue, it appears to wish to discuss it within the framework of an all-European security conference, which would not be organized around the two military blocs. Given the great difficulty that East European states would have in speaking out with genuinely independent voices in such a conference, and the greater pluralism of the Western or non-Communist countries, it is not clear that a conference of this kind could escape becoming at least partly an instrument of Soviet foreign policy. The Soviet Union is vigorously pursuing people-to-people measures on the subject of the European security conference through a special committee of the Central Committee of the Communist Party of the Soviet Union, and is engaging in other activities of this kind that are reminiscent of the "popular front from below" of the 1930s. Although the United States and Canada are included as participants, the measures proposed for the conference, such as agreements not to use force, could be the

81

opening wedges in campaigns designed to remove the American military presence from Europe, and thus, the important links between Western Europe and the United States that prevent the Soviet Union from becoming the hegemonial power on the continent, almost regardless of its intentions. The dissuasion strategy could provide an aura of confidence within which these possible adverse influences may be minimized. By linking removal of QRAs and Pershings to removal of Soviet IRBMs, MRBMs, and SRBMs, the Soviet Union may be forced to negotiate on a more equitable basis.

SALT. The dissuasion strategy is consistent with the arms limitations reached in the SALT agreements of May 1972. The one factor that did not achieve sufficient examination during the SALT agreements involved the targetting capabilities of the Polaris/Poseidon fleet under a dissuasion strategy that might require up to 25 percent of the U.S. fleet capabilities. This conceivably might stretch planned American targetting capabilities, although it would not clearly exceed them.

6
Alternative Futures

Factors Affecting Dissuasion

In some respects, the situation confronting NATO is critical. The present situation of NATO is militarily untenable and cannot withstand an intense crisis. Current military weaknesses and provocative weapons systems both facilitate a decision to generate a crisis and provide grounds for provocation by the Soviet Union in crisis-prone circumstances. On the other hand, despite the clear insufficiencies at present and the possibilities for further erosion inherent in the domestic political situations of the United States and the Western European countries, dissuasion works and is consistent with détente. This may be a mere illusion, for there has been no recent challenge and no recent incentive, given the world position of the Soviet Union, for it to launch a challenge. But the stability of NATO is a fact of political perception in the West.

Any suggestion for change introduces uncertainties, for the professed reasons for the change may merely mask the actual reasons or may set off a chain of uncontrollable events. Moreover, as dangerous as the Pershing missile force may be from the standpoint of stability during crises, it is at least a visible symbol of American nuclear presence during this period of détente.

The fear of change is exacerbated by the diplomacy of the Nixon administration, which, because of its emphasis up to the present on relations with the Russians and Chinese, leaves Western Europe in uncertainty. Our NATO allies, and France in particular, fear that the United States and the Soviet Union may deal over their heads. Bilateral U.S.-U.S.S.R. statements that pointedly ignore the principle of self-determination in Europe add to their unease. Lack of sufficient and sustained diplomatic contact between them and the United States produces uncertainty with respect to Nixon's world objectives and stability of purpose.

Is a Kissinger-type "multipolarity" a signal of an American retreat from the world? Although Nixon has explicitly distinguished Europe from Asia with respect to direct involvement of American forces and has, moreover, shown his stability even in the case of Asia by his willingness to engage in unpopular bombing in Vietnam in an effort to secure for the Thieu government some reasonable chance for perseverance, he is not given full credit for this performance. Today, as at the time of Korea, American attention to Asia worries Europeans that the United States will be diverted from Europe. Although this author believes that a failure of American will in Asia would much more likely set off internal political processes that would diminish our interest in and cooperation with Europe, European opinion seems to differ on this point.

If dissuasion would be a cure for the present instability, it is by no means clear that dissuasion can be adopted by NATO. Moreover, even if dissuasion is adopted, it may not be a long-term solution for the problems of NATO. Although dissuasion has much political merit in the ways in which it affects political decisions in the WTO, its military implications rest on the present balance of forces in Europe and could be offset to a considerable extent either by further deterioration in the NATO situation or improvements in the WTO situation. Alternatively, major technological improvements, for instance, in the production of cheap and efficient antitank weapons, might resurrect a situation of defensive stability in Europe, even given the current low political support in both the United States and in Europe for the maintenance of adequate military forces.

There are a number of factors in the current situation that provide NATO with time. The Soviet Union seems highly preoccupied with its long China border. The Sino-American détente provides an additional element of deterrence to the Soviet Union against solving the Chinese problem by force. In addition, the apparently rapid improvements in Chinese nuclear weaponry that in January 1973 led Richard Helms, the outgoing director of the CIA, to refer to China as a major world power [1] further strengthen that element of deterrence. Although too strong a

---

[1] *New York Times,* January 9, 1973.

relationship between China and the United States might well thrust the Soviet Union into a thoroughly defensive and hostile set of policies, the current level of détente leads the Soviet Union instead to seek to reemphasize the joint leading roles in the world of the Soviet Union and the United States by conferences such as SALT and on European security. Although it would be extremely difficult to footnote this point, the increasing acceptability of the United States to the Soviet Union in European security conferences may result less from European insistence on this point than from the Soviet requirement of continually reemphasizing the joint leading role of the two powers—the very factor that gives rise to some suspicion in Western Europe of American motives.

The attempt by the Soviet Union to maintain this type of relationship with the United States provides NATO with some bargaining space in the pursuit of military stabilization in Europe. It may be one of the factors that helped produce the recent German agreement and provides an additional reason why Willy Brandt may be extremely wary of any major changes in the present situation. At the same time, however, by emphasizing Russian participation in the affairs of Western as well as Eastern Europe, the developments move subtly against the rationale of NATO and may impair its long-term political support. Thus, every step into this unknown future appears double-edged. This would be especially the case if the military situation of NATO vis-à-vis the WTO weakens as a consequence of measures of détente and military reductions.

As recently as January 1973, Soviet moves indicated that military reductions in Europe would be modest in quantitative size.[2] This indicates an unwillingness to plunge too rapidly into the unknown or to run the risk that the Soviet Union might have to impose the Brezhnev Doctrine again. Yet despite the deemphasis of the Brezhnev Doctrine at the present time, it constitutes a dagger pointed at the vitals of NATO. The recent Yugoslav treaty asserted the right of both Yugoslavia and the Soviet Union to pursue their own path to socialism. However, if the Soviet Union defines the Yugoslav path as something other than socialism, there is perhaps an implied right of pressure if not of overt intervention. Conceivably a leftist coalition in France or in Italy might lead to the definition of the situations in either country as socialist. Provided that this process was not too abrupt, consultations between Russia and either country might establish a presumption of Russian interest in

---

[2] See article by Hedrick Smith, *New York Times,* January 19, 1973.

internal developments in these countries that does not presently exist. The subtle and complex political implications of this need not be spelled out here. In any event, these remarks are purely speculative, reenforcing the opinion expressed earlier of the double-edged character of all these new developments.

The choice seems clear to this author. Even though each of the NATO members may perceive the present situation as preferable to any potential solution proposed by any of the others given the uncertainties of any such solution, the present situation is inherently unstable. By one means or another we will reinvigorate NATO or we will move to one of a number of alternate futures in which NATO is deemphasized or abandoned. We will not remain where we are. A number of these potential futures are discussed below. The reader may decide for himself which of them appears more likely in the absence of a reinvigorated NATO.

Disengagement

To the extent that the United States should desire to pursue a policy of disengagement in Europe, it is necessary to go slowly and carefully in parallel with the Soviet Union. It would not be sufficient merely to dismantle NATO and the Warsaw Pact. The U.S.S.R. would also have to withdraw from Comecon, for the absence of the United States from Europe in both a military and an economic sense would make the Soviet Union a power of hegemonial capability on the Eurasian land mass. British policy throughout the nineteenth century was designed to prevent the emergence of such a dominant power on the mainland of Europe, and today the United States needs to play an analogous role within the framework of a larger world arena. Yet, it is likely to be most difficult, if not actually impossible, to convince the Soviet Union of this. There is some reason to believe that the current Soviet political leadership is naive.[3] This author believes it underestimates to a considerable extent the divisive tendencies that would be set off in East Europe by an accelerated demobilization of NATO. Even though the Czechoslovak crisis of 1968 has alerted the Soviet leadership somewhat to divisive tendencies in East Europe, it still seems to seriously underestimate this potentiality. Too rapid a removal of Soviet forces from East Europe

---

[3] This estimate is based on inferences from extensive discussions of the relevant problems of Europe with Eastern Europeans and Russians.

might produce a new series of revolts that would force the Soviet Union back in, and in even a heavier-handed fashion than was employed in Czechoslovakia in 1968. This would very seriously set back détente.

Precisely because of the dangers arising from too rapid a dismantling of the Soviet presence in East Europe, too avid support for such measures by Westerners might appear to the Russians as Machiavellian maneuvers designed to disrupt the socialist sphere. On the other hand, given the dangers to the Soviet system in too rapid a reduction of forces in the East, Soviet proposals seeming to promise this result should be looked at at least as suspiciously as the Trojans should have looked at the Trojan horse. This is why bloc disengagement may be one of the most difficult and intricate management problems we have ever faced, even assuming the best of will on both sides. If this is so, the continued maintenance of both NATO and the Warsaw Pact, although perhaps within the framework of mutual balanced forces reduction, may be essential to European stability and détente.

A New Europe?

There can be little doubt under current circumstances that NATO is essential to the security of West Europe. This need not be the case for all time, even if the Soviet Union remains in some sense hostile. The population of Western Europe is greater than that of the United States and the economic potential is great. However, there is no single West European power of sufficient size, military strength, and political credibility around whose focus an effective coalition might be built. Nor does the new Europe yet exist except perhaps in embryo.

Conceivably the movement toward European unity might produce sufficient military cohesion and political credibility to change the current requirement for a strong NATO. However, in the absence of the United States, this Europe would need a nuclear weapons system that could be used credibly in the interest of each of its members. The present British and French forces are too miniscule to meet this need. They provide little potential protection to Germany, Italy, or the northern countries. Moreover, the political controls on them would not meet the needs of these countries in a crisis. If a genuine European nuclear force were to evolve, depending upon its character and the circumstances of control, this might substitute for American nuclear protection. If a more unified

87

Europe displayed a willingness to build such a force, the United States might well consider transmitting the technological knowledge required to increase the economical feasibility of the force.

The Arms Race in a Multipolar World

Depending upon developments elsewhere in the world—the emergence of China, Japan, and possibly Brazil as major states—we might be able to move toward a more decentralized structure of world politics in which the nuclear arms race is somewhat deemphasized. There are several reasons why this might be the case. Although many argue that the missile-carrying submarine fleet is invulnerable, this invulnerability is only to the antisubmarine warfare methods currently in use or development in the United States. We cannot be sure what may be true of Soviet capabilities. Every particular military system has vulnerabilities. Therefore, when two major nuclear states face each other, each likes a wide, rather than merely a thin, margin of safety, for the balance is subject to unknown factors. This fuels the qualitative arms race, for, given the approximately seven-year lead-time factor in major weapons system deployment, no nation can afford to run a substantial risk of a technological breakthrough by the other side in a two-power race.

The proliferation of major, protected, and well-controlled nuclear systems to other stable, bureaucratic states would dampen this problem. In such a nuclear world, any state that engages in a nuclear first strike against any other nuclear power would have to face the rest of the nuclear states and would already have demonstrated its dangerous characteristics. At best, the other nuclear states would now engage in a hectic arms race for self-protection and, at worst, they would attempt to eliminate a proven dangerous actor. Therefore, unless a single nuclear state is in a position to conduct a first strike against all of them simultaneously, the move against any particular one, everything else being equal, hardly seems to commend itself. Under these circumstances, the fear of a first strike in a crisis would be lower than in a two-power situation. Therefore, the fears fuelling the qualitative arms race would be diminished. Apart from the arms race itself, these factors might also feed back into the political conditions of the international system, creating more security and making it easier to search for agreements that might further transform the modes of international behavior.

Even More Radical Alternatives

If NATO can develop an effective strategy such as the dissuasion strategy that promotes a climate of confidence in the NATO area, if NATO can move forward toward détente, if it can act to reduce the dangers and the costs of the arms race, and if it can maintain both American and West European security while a transition to new forms of structure and process for the international system is managed, then a climate of stability will exist within which more radical measures for transforming the international system can be explored. It is very important that these be explored by people who are not ideologues and who will pay close attention to their potential dangers as well as their possible potential advantages. I will do little more than name a few of the alternatives that are worth this kind of exploration.

Open Laboratories. The qualitative arms race, for instance, is fuelled by uncertainty. If all laboratories in both the Soviet Union and the United States were mutually open, it would pay neither party to develop a destabilizing weapons system, for its research on the subject would be provided free of cost to the potential antagonist. There are obvious problems with this proposal. How would one be assured that one really had access to all the classified information in the weapons area? How would one be satisfied that the Soviet Union, which we believe is technologically behind us in weapons development, would not accept the inspection system only until it had exhausted our technological knowledge? We cannot begin to explore these serious questions until we get down to the hard details of the problems and examine them carefully.

Agreements on Revolutionary Change. Is there any form of agreement that can be reached between the United States and the Soviet Union that would set limitations on the kinds of revolutionary changes that would be allowed to take place elsewhere in the world? Obviously the Soviet Union would be concerned about a principle that would exclude one-party states universally. The United States needs to be concerned about a major increase in the number of one-party states, even if they are independent or relatively so, for too many such changes might create too hostile a climate for political democracy in either West Europe or the United States. On the other hand, the United States has little interest in preventing the spread elsewhere in the world of socialism as an

89

economic system. The United States and the Soviet Union, and perhaps someday China, could dampen international political conflict by agreeing that none would interfere in revolutionary movements outside of certain defined areas, provided opposition parties were permitted to exist and certain types of personal freedoms continued.[4] One's first thought is that the Soviet Union would unhesitatingly reject this proposal, but maybe such a conclusion is premature. Possibly if we explore this in some detail, and as a compensation withdraw forceful American opposition to socialization, we may dampen the risks involved in revolutionary change.

A Final Comment

The dissuasion strategy provides a means for insuring the political viability of Western Europe under contemporary conditions. It could be viewed as an end in itself, but it might also be treated as a transitional stage in the development of a better world order. It is precisely because the dissuasion strategy would work so well that it can provide a framework within which other alternatives can safely be explored. Unlike the present situation of NATO, in which the adequacy of strategy and doctrine is subject to serious doubt, the dissuasion strategy would permit that kind of search for new alternatives that the confidently strong can take.

---

[4] This is contrary to the Joint American-Chinese communiqué issued from Shanghai, February 27, 1972, deploring the concept of spheres of influence. *Peking Review,* March 3, 1972, p. 5.

Bibliography

To obtain as good a first-hand account as possible of the perspectives of those who made the important American decisions in the late-war and early-postwar period, their personal accounts must be read. Among the most useful are:

Acheson, Dean Gooderham. *Present at the Creation: My Years in the State Department.* New York: W. W. Norton and Co., 1969.

Bohlen, Charles Eustis. *The Transformation of American Foreign Policy.* New York: W. W. Norton and Co., 1969.

Byrnes, James Francis. *Speaking Frankly.* New York: Harper and Row, 1947.

Churchill, Sir Winston Leonard Spencer. *The Second World War: Triumph and Tragedy,* vol. 4. London: Cassell, 1951.

————. *The Second World War: Closing the Ring,* vol. 5. London: Cassell, 1952.

Clay, Lucius du Bignon. *Decision in Germany.* Garden City, New York: Doubleday and Co., 1950.

Forrestal, James. *The Forrestal Diaries.* Edited by Walter Millis. New York: Viking Press, 1951.

Kennan, George Frost. *Memoirs: 1925-1950.* Boston: Little, Brown and Co., 1967.

Sherwood, Robert Emmet. *Roosevelt and Hopkins: An Intimate History.* New York: Harper and Row, 1948.

Stettinius, Edward Reilly. *Roosevelt and the Russians: The Yalta Conference.* Edited by Walter Johnson. Garden City, New York: Doubleday and Co., 1949.

Truman, Harry S. *Memoirs: Year of Decisions,* vol. 1. Garden City, New York: Doubleday and Co., 1955.

————. *Memoirs: Years of Trial and Hope,* vol. 2. Garden City, New York: Doubleday and Co., 1956.

Vandenberg, Arthur Hendrick. *The Private Papers of Senator Vandenberg.* Edited by Arthur H. Vandenberg, Jr. Boston: Houghton-Mifflin Co., 1952.

Fair-minded analyses of the events of the early period may be found in:

Feis, Herbert. *From Trust to Terror: The Onset of the Cold War, 1945-1950.* New York: W. W. Norton and Co., 1970.

Reitzel, William; Kaplan, Morton A.; and Coblenz, Constance G. *United States Foreign Policy: 1945-1955.* Washington, D. C.: The Brookings Institution, 1956.

Snell, John Leslie, ed. *The Meaning of Yalta: Big Three Diplomacy and the New Balance of Power.* Baton Rouge: Louisiana State University Press, 1956.

Theoharis, Athan George. *The Yalta Myths: An Issue in U.S. Politics, 1945-1955.* Columbia: University of Missouri Press, 1970.

Revisionist accounts would be well represented by:

Alperovitz, Gar. *Atomic Diplomacy: Hiroshima and Potsdam.* New York: Simon and Schuster, 1965.

Kolko, Gabriel. *The Roots of American Foreign Policy: An Analysis of Power and Purpose.* Boston: Beacon Press, 1969.

Kolko, Gabriel, and Kolko, Joyce. *The Limits of Power: The World and United States Foreign Policy, 1945-1954.* New York: Harper and Row, 1972.

Maddox, Robert James. *The New Left and the Origin of the Cold War.* Princeton, New Jersey: Princeton University Press, 1973. A critique of the revisionists.

Personal accounts of the Kennedy years include:

Schlesinger, Arthur Meier. *A Thousand Days: John F. Kennedy in the White House.* Boston: Houghton-Mifflin Co., 1965.

Sorensen, Theodore C. *Kennedy.* New York: Harper and Row, 1965.

Insights into Russian perspectives may be obtained from such personal records as:

Dedijer, Vladimir. *Tito.* New York: Simon and Schuster, 1953.

Djilas, Milovan. *Conversations with Stalin.* Translated by Michael B. Petrovich. New York: Harcourt, Brace and World, 1962.

Russian military policies, including nuclear, are to be found in:

Garthoff, Raymond L. *Soviet Strategy in the Nuclear Age.* New York: Praeger Publishers, 1958.

Holst, Johan Jorgen. "Comparative U.S. and Soviet Deployments, Doctrines, and Arms Limitation." In *SALT: Problems and Prospects.* Edited by Morton A. Kaplan. Morristown, New Jersey: General Learning Press, 1972.

Horelick, Arnold L., and Rush, Myron. *Strategic Power and Soviet Foreign Policy.* Chicago: University of Chicago Press, 1966.

Wolfe, Thomas W. *Soviet Power and Europe: 1945-1970.* Baltimore: Johns Hopkins Press, 1970.

Scholarly studies of Russian diplomacy useful to understanding European problems include:

Shulman, Marshall Darrow. *Stalin's Foreign Policy Reappraised.* Cambridge: Harvard University Press, 1963.

Ulam, Adam Bruno. *Expansion and Coexistence: The History of Soviet Foreign Policy, 1917-1967.* New York: Praeger Publishers, 1968.

―――. *The Rivals: America and Russia since World War II.* New York: Viking Press, 1971.

The quotations on the subject of German rearmament are taken from the *New York Times* and the *Washington Post.* A good scholarly study of this problem may be found in:

Sharfman, Peter. "International Negotiations Preceding the Rearmament of West Germany: 1949-1955." Ph.D. dissertation, University of Chicago, 1972.

A good study of de Gaulle and of French policy is found in:

Kulski, W. W. *De Gaulle and the World: The Foreign Policy of the Fifth French Republic.* Syracuse: Syracuse University Press, 1966.

A good study of German policy is found in:

Hanrieder, Wolfram. *The Stable Crisis: Two Decades of German Foreign Policy.* New York: Harper and Row, 1970.

Early studies of NATO and of problems concerning NATO nuclear strategy after the emergence of a Soviet strategic force include:

Buchan, Alastair. *NATO in the 1960s: The Implications of Interdependence.* New York: Praeger Publishers, 1960.

Knorr, Klaus, ed. *NATO and American Security.* Princeton: Princeton University Press, 1959.

Knorr, Klaus, and Read, Thornton, eds. *Limited Strategic War.* New York: Praeger Publishers, 1962.

More recent studies, dealing as well with problems of conventional defense and "pause" strategies, include:

Halperin, Morton H. *Defense Strategies for the Seventies.* Boston: Little, Brown, and Co., 1971.

Pfaltzgraff, Robert L., Jr. *The Atlantic Community: A Complex Imbalance.* New York: Van Nostrand-Reinhold Co., 1969.

For a view of the conventional defensibility of NATO sharply differing from mine, see:

Enthoven, Alain, and Smith, K. Wayne. *How Much is Enough? Shaping the Defense Program, 1961-1969.* New York: Harper and Row, 1971.

For changes in the strategic balance as they affect NATO, see:

Kaplan, Morton A. "SALT and the International System." In *SALT: Problems and Prospects.* Edited by Morton A. Kaplan. Morristown, New Jersey: General Learning Press, 1972.

Kintner, William R., ed. *Safeguard: Why the ABM Makes Sense.* New York: Hawthorn Books, 1969.

For contrasting views, see:

Bundy, McGeorge. "To Cap the Volcano." *Foreign Affairs,* vol. 48 (October 1969).

York, Herbert F. "Military Technology and National Security." *Scientific American,* August 1969.

For a discussion of the reasons why automatic deterrence systems would be more likely to reveal the lack of will of the deterrer than to deter an aggressor, see the discussion of commitment in:

Kaplan, Morton A. "A Note on Game Theory and Bargaining." In *New Approaches to International Relations.* Edited by Morton A. Kaplan. New York: St. Martin's Press, 1968.